American Indian and White Relations to 1830
Needs and Opportunities for Study

The Institute of Early American History and Culture is sponsored jointly by the College of William and Mary and Colonial Williamsburg, Incorporated

NEEDS AND OPPORTUNITIES FOR STUDY SERIES

Early American Science
WHITFIELD J. BELL, JR.

American Indian and White Relations to 1830
WILLIAM N. FENTON

American Indian and
White Relations to 1830

Needs & Opportunities for Study

AN ESSAY BY

William N. Fenton

&

A BIBLIOGRAPHY BY

L. H. Butterfield, Wilcomb E. Washburn, and William N. Fenton

Published for

THE INSTITUTE OF EARLY AMERICAN HISTORY
AND CULTURE, WILLIAMSBURG, VIRGINIA

by

THE UNIVERSITY OF NORTH CAROLINA PRESS

CHAPEL HILL

1957

119242

MANUFACTURED IN THE UNITED STATES OF AMERICA BY
THE WILLIAM BYRD PRESS, INCORPORATED, RICHMOND, VIRGINIA

The Institute Conferences

DURING the academic year 1952-1953 the Institute of Early American History and Culture held a series of conferences in Williamsburg to encourage a broadening of historical studies into fields where relatively little original research has been carried on or where new approaches to old problems challenge investigators. The first of these conferences on needs and opportunities for study was devoted to Early American Science, with Whitfield J. Bell, Jr., as the authority. His essay and bibliography, published under that title, appeared in 1955. The material of the second conference, on Early American Law, led by Mark Howe, is in preparation.

The essay in the present volume was read by William N. Fenton at the conference on Early American Indian and White Relations, held on February 19, 1953. In the light of discussion by the participants the author revised his paper for publication. Meanwhile a bibliography, designed for students of history and ethnology, was compiled jointly by Lyman H. Butterfield, Wilcomb E. Washburn, and Mr. Fenton. It is hoped that both the essay and the bibliography will stimulate graduate students to explore this field and will aid more mature scholars as well.

The Institute is continuing these conferences, the most recent one being on Early American Architecture, held in Williamsburg on November 17, 1956.

A little *Key* may open a *Box,*
where lies a *bunch* of *Keyes.*
                    —Roger Williams,
A Key into the Language of America
(London, 1643)

Foreword

FEW aspects of early American history have attracted more attention than the relations, sometimes peaceful but often warlike, between the white settlers and the Indians. This colorful relationship is a part of our heritage, although intellectual historians debate the form it takes in the white psyche. The literature on the subject is enormous, even in specialized fields such as captivity narratives. But despite the interest and despite the myriad volumes that have dealt with Indian-white relations, only the base has been laid for a properly full and critical study.

Two separate approaches have been traditional in Indian studies. The earliest and most persistent has been the approach of the historian, antiquarian, and man of letters. Armed with the traditions and assumptions of Western European culture, the humanist has dealt with the Indian as a curiosity, or more commonly as an environmental influence, either beneficial or harmful, on white development.

In the mid-nineteenth century a new tradition of Indian studies arose. Lewis H. Morgan and the men who followed him in studies now termed "ethnological" or "anthropological," attempted to see the Indian in terms of his own society. The scientists in the new tradition were gradually able to show that the structure of an Indian society was complicated and that Indian societies were of extremely diverse types. But most of all they were able to show that the humanists frequently had not been discussing Indians who existed or had existed, but Indians recreated to fit the terms of the humanists' society.

Now we are at the point where these two traditions can profitably be brought together to illuminate not merely the Indian in terms of white society or the Indian in terms of his own society, but each in his own terms *and* in terms of the other. The study of Indian-white relations must encompass both self-knowledge and knowledge of others.

It is hoped that this survey and bibliography will encourage penetration of existing academic barriers between the humanities and the sciences, and a union of scholars who struggle toward greater understanding of Indian-white relations in both camps. William N. Fenton, who here presents a plea for "ethnohistory," as the new amalgam is called, has had a varied career in teaching, government, and museum work. As an anthropologist whose work has been principally among the Iroquois, he has attempted to work "upstream," applying present-day ethnological data and principles to the historic past, insofar as it is validly possible to do so. Shortly before giving the paper printed in this book he left the staff of the Bureau of American Ethnology of the Smithsonian Institution to become executive secretary of the Division of Anthropology and Psychology of the National Research Council. At present he is assistant commissioner for the New York State Museum and Science Service in Albany.

Following his talk, Mr. Fenton supplied Lyman H. Butterfield, then director of the Institute, with a set of bibliography cards listing important ethnological works on the subject of the American Indian. Mr. Butterfield then devised the present organizational scheme of the bibliography and selected works that would supplement Mr. Fenton's references and provide adequate coverage in the non-ethnological fields. When Mr. Butterfield left for Boston to take on his time-consuming duties as editor-in-chief of the Adams Papers, the bibliography was still unfinished. Desiring to get the work before the public as soon as possible, Mr. Butterfield and I asked Wilcomb E. Washburn, research associate at the Institute, to complete the bibliography and see it through the press. Since Mr. Washburn has been working for several years on a study of the legal and moral justifications for dispossessing the American Indian, we felt he was well qualified to finish the task. He made additions to the bibliography, corresponded with experts in the field concerning other changes and additions, and prepared Mr. Fenton's paper for the press. In his dual capacity as revisor and editor Mr. Washburn has made a noteworthy contribution to the project.

All of us who worked on the bibliography wish to express our appreciation to the outside readers who gave so generously of their time and advice. Valuable additions and criticisms, from which the bibliography has greatly benefited, were received from Kenneth E. Kidd, Royal

Ontario Museum, Toronto; Stanley M. Pargellis, Newberry Library, Chicago; Roy Harvey Pearce, Ohio State University, Columbus; Howard H. Peckham, William L. Clements Library, Ann Arbor; Dwight Smith, Miami University, Oxford, Ohio; John R. Swanton, Newton, Massachusetts; Sol Tax, University of Chicago; Erminie Wheeler-Voegelin, Indiana University, Bloomington; and Anthony F. C. Wallace, Philadelphia, Pennsylvania. Similarly we are in debt to the staffs of numerous historical societies, state and federal archival agencies, and libraries for their kindness in answering our queries about manuscript holdings.

Next, a note of warning. Mr. Butterfield has expressed the purpose of the Institute's "Needs and Opportunities for Study" series in his foreword to Whitfield J. Bell, Jr.'s *Early American Science* (Williamsburg, 1955). Briefly, each of the books in this series is intended as a kind of *vade-mecum* to the subject with which it deals. None attempts to provide a systematic account of its subject or a complete bibliography of it. The primary aim of the series is to serve the needs of graduate students and those directing their studies, and thereby to foster better research in fields that offer many attractions, once the barrier of unfamiliarity has been broken down. For the student of history, the present work provides a guide to important ethnological literature. For the student of ethnology it provides a guide to important historical literature.

The bibliography which accompanies Mr. Fenton's paper is divided into seven categories—the last with seven subdivisions, as the table of contents sets forth. The numerous divisions are unnecessary and, indeed, antagonistic to the purpose of a formal bibliography of Indian-white relations. However, they are made deliberately in order to break up the vast literature into categories which will attract prospective research students into the field. We hope that the reader will bear in mind our purpose if he decides to use the book merely as a bibliographical tool.

The reader will find many items in the bibliography which could have been placed in different categories, and will think of many others which might have been added or omitted. We hope he will not be disturbed to see items in the bibliography dealing with South Sea Islanders or Indians of the American Southwest. The student of Indian-white relations in Eastern North America before 1830 is at a disadvantage because some of the tribes he must understand are now extinct, and most have experienced such extreme cultural change that generalizations based on their modern descendants must be handled with caution. Hence the inclusion of studies of property concepts, legal assumptions, ethics, etc., among Indians remote from the place and period of primary concern. A few classics and basic texts in the field of anthropology have been added with a similar disregard for their immediate pertinence. Such items are for the historian unversed in anthropology who could profit by an elementary survey of the basic principles of that science. Other works not immediately related to early American history are listed because their authors are mentioned by Mr. Fenton in his paper. The bibliography is intended to be comprehensive enough to eliminate the need for footnotes in his essay.

The change in status of the Indian inhabitants of America from powerful equals to dependent wards has inevitably made it difficult for historians to appreciate the full significance of Indian-white relations in the colonial period. It is hoped that publication of this guide to further study in the field will not only illuminate this important relationship in our past, but provide historical perspective for racial conflicts on our increasingly confined planet.

LESTER J. CAPPON, Director

Williamsburg, August, 1956

Contents

Indian and White Relations in Eastern North America:

A Common Ground for History and Ethnology

Indian and White Relations in Eastern North America:

A Common Ground for History and Ethnology

BY WILLIAM N. FENTON

I

IT IS in the spirit of Dekanisora, speaker of the Five Nations, who called on Governor Spotswood here at Williamsburg supposedly before 1720, that I have come to your fire to polish the "Chain of Friendship" between the ethnologists and the historians. I stand here therefore with the white wampum of friendship in my hands and address to you three words only of requickening—first, to wipe away your tears for those who have gone the long trail since our last meeting, second, to remove the obstructions from your ears so that you may hear my message, and third, to clear your throats of any bitterness that may subsist between us that you may reply later with a clear mind. One by one my words will pass across the fire to you—a string of wampum to attest each word, which you may grasp firmly and rack up on a pole to remind you of what I have said, that you may also put my words under your heads as a pillow and sleep on them before you answer another day. Now my message is on its way to you.

I have just spoken in the manner of the old Iroquois orators, with some confidence because after being conventionally trained as an ethnologist the old men of the Six Nations proceeded to make a man of me, as they promised the colonial governors they would their sons on numerous occasions, and of late years I have worked beside the historians. The anthropologists, my colleagues, have twice invited me to lecture to them on "The Training of Historical Ethnologists in America" and on the materials, theory, and practice of historical study. It is not quite a novel experience, therefore, for an ethnologist to attempt to explain to historians how historical ethnology is practiced, especially since the Newberry Library Conference on Indian Studies brought a group of anthropologists and historians together for a day of talk in 1952. The present meeting is an example of further cooperation between the disciplines.

Toward this end the present paper is organized under five heads: Indian ethnography for historians; the literature of the council fire (historical materials on Indian and white relations); upstreaming, the method of ethnohistory; condolence and calumet, the drama of forest diplomacy; and common tasks, an agenda for mutual assistance.

II

Ethnography is that branch of cultural anthropology which treats cultures systematically in time and space. It differs from archeology mainly in that it derives its perspective from, and is mainly concerned with, the ways of life of living peoples. If the ethnographer is not the observer himself, he attempts to arrange the observations of earlier explorers, missionaries, colonial officials, captives, and others who saw the people in question and who left written records for posterity. What distinguishes the ethnographer from the historian, however, is a concern with the languages and cultures of preliterate, or "primitive," peoples and a classificatory sense for describing them in terms of themselves. In fact, until quite recently I could say with confidence that ethnology is the cultural history of primitive peoples. This is no longer true because the development in Britain and America of social anthropology has extended the methods of analysis developed by Bronislaw Malinowski, A. R. Radcliffe-Brown, and Ralph Linton from preliterate social systems to modern societies. But social anthropology concerns us in the present paper only insofar as in common with historical ethnology it stresses field work with living societies and derives its method of systematic observation and analysis from real people. Historical ethnologists such as James Mooney and John R. Swanton, in common with Frank G. Speck, Alfred L. Kroeber, Robert H. Lowie, and Clark Wissler, have all made field trips to societies of living Indians where they have perhaps acquired a working knowledge of one or more related Indian languages. When they turn to historical source materials in libraries, therefore, they interpret what they read in terms of what they know of living people. Kroeber himself has complained that ethnologists have gone to the field by choice to escape the drudgery of the library.

Summers in the field and winters in the library have comprised the ethnologist's yearly round of activity and so he measures ecological time for himself as surely as he notes among the Eskimo winter fishing and taking of sea mammals on the ice, and summer removal to hunt caribou on the barren grounds. During the approximately seventy-five years since its founding in 1879, the staff of the Bureau of American Ethnology of the Smithsonian Institution has concerned itself with ethnic entities—the carriers of cultures—their identities, locations, contacts, and movements. Research in the Library of the Bureau has made the Smithsonian the final place of appeal on such matters, sometimes to the dismay of the staff who have been known to spend a third of their time answering the letters of school children, scout masters, teachers, local historians, writers, journalists, and, above all, citizens. But performing spot information research has a certain cumulative value which Frederick W. Hodge captured in the Bureau's famous *Handbook of American Indians* (*Bulletin* 30, 1907-1910). And from the beginning of a long career John R. Swanton kept a helpful eye on the historian and general scholar, giving us a substantial series of historical monographs and regional summaries. *Indian Tribes of the Lower Mississippi Valley and Adjacent Coast of the Gulf of Mexico* (*Bulletin* 43, 1911) contains about all that is known of the Natchez; it was followed by a series of tall monographs on the Creek Indians and their neighbors; his *Final Report of the United States DeSoto Expedition Commission* (1939) is now a collector's item; Swanton put a capstone to his work with *Indians of the Southeastern United States* (*Bulletin* 137, 1946); and added a finial to the capstone with *The Indian Tribes of North America* (*Bulletin* 145, 1952). The latter work is a tribal map of the continent and the text classifies tribal entities by states. Each tribal entity follows a key arranged by synonymy, racial and linguistic con-

nections, location, subdivisions, villages, history, population, and con-
nections in which they have been noted. The individual sketches lack
references, but there is a substantial bibliography. Swanton's achieve-
ments in the history, ethnography, and linguistics of the Southeast are
so great that there is danger of forgetting his colleagues.

James Mooney, the fiery-haired Irishman who once worked on the
newspaper of Wissler's father in Indiana and started out to list all the
books in the libraries of the world, soon turned his talents to a tribal
synonymy which grew into Hodge's *Handbook*. Mooney had two great
loves—history and Indians—and he wrote felicitously. He was not satis-
fied to "muse on nations passed away," nor did he content himself with
the Bureau Library where the volumes contain many notes in his hand,
but he sought out and befriended the descendants of the Siouan rem-
nants up and down the Piedmont. *Siouan Tribes of the East (Bulletin
22, 1894)* attains a historical and literary quality seldom reached in
ethnographic writing. But the Cherokee were Mooney's favorite people
and he was their champion. *Myths of the Cherokee* (1900), *Sacred
Formulas of the Cherokees* (1892), and with Frans M. Olbrechts, *The
Swimmer Manuscript (Bulletin 99, 1932)* present only a fraction of
Mooney's long participation in the life of the Eastern Cherokee, for
much remains in manuscript. Mooney took out a few years to write
an even more famous classic, *The Ghost Dance Religion and the Sioux
Outbreak of 1890* (1897), which is very nearly a "first" in applied
anthropology.

Without Mooney we might fall back on the late Frank G. Speck
who aroused great admiration in Swanton, was beloved by his students
and colleagues, and who was acclaimed by Algonquians, Siouans, and
Iroquoians alike, from Labrador to Louisiana, as one of their own. In
his heyday Speck used to treat his students by taking them on forays
into the Delaware and Virginia swamps and to the Great Smokies of
North Carolina where they combined field collecting in natural history
with recovering the ancient hunting and fishing lore, ethnobotany, and
bird lore among the Nanticoke, Rappahannock, Chickahominy, and
Cherokee, not to mention the Delaware, Abenaki, and Cayuga in the
north. Speck's students were naturalists then as well as ethnologists and
a few of them, like Theodore Stern, have a real historical sense. John
Witthoft is the heir to Mooney among the Cherokee, and his brief

papers on Cherokee herbalism and birdlore convey the spirit of the people and their culture more nearly than William Gilbert's monograph, *The Eastern Cherokees* (1944).

We may note with pleasure that the tidewater Algonquians, who have over the years resisted study because their history is long, tangled, and obscure and their scattered descendants almost completely deculturated and mixed with other races, are now represented in the literature by substantial reports from students of Speck. Professor Maurice A. Mook has published a series of ethnohistorical studies on the Virginia and Carolina aboriginal populations in the *American Anthropologist,* the *William and Mary College Quarterly,* and the *Journal of the Washington Academy of Sciences;* and the *Proceedings of the American Philosophical Society* (1952) carried Professor Theodore Stern's "Chickahominy: The Changing Culture of a Virginia Indian Community." All of these ethnologists would acknowledge that their work has been enhanced by the labors of local historians such as C. J. Milling, whose *Red Carolinians* (1940) has systematized the sources on the ethnic groups of two states. If the tradition of Mooney and Speck has made a hobby of finding the remnant tribes and recalling the last vestiges of Indian culture, William Harlen Gilbert, Jr. of the Library of Congress has seen the Wesorts and others as out-casted groups, like the marginal tribes of India, and he has located and catalogued *Surviving Indian Groups of the Eastern United States* (Smithsonian *Annual Report for 1948*) from the Brass Ankles of South Carolina to the Mashpee of Gay Head.

Present political boundaries which may serve history and archeology mean little as compared with language family and dialectical distribution for classifying ethnic entities in Eastern North America. From the publication of John Wesley Powell's *Indian Linguistic Families of America North of Mexico* (1892), the Powell map has dominated the thinking of American ethnologists. And the culture area approach, first advanced by Wissler in *The American Indian: An Introduction to the Anthropology of the New World* (1917), has attained remarkable refinement under the hand of Kroeber who demonstrated that the *Cultural and Natural Areas of Native North America* (1939), when mapped, exhibit some nice concordances of language, culture, and environment.

To stay within the limits of our topic, "Indian and White Relations in Eastern North America," we need but consider four language families: the Algonquian, Iroquoian, Siouan, and Muskhogean. Seen historically, it was the Algonquians who welcomed the Virginia colony and greeted the Pilgrim Fathers, by whom they were soon extinguished or driven from New England for the glory of God; the Virginia Siouans felt the first impact of the western movement; the Iroquoians and the mobile Algonquians resisted it; and for a time among the Muskhogean Creek and Iroquoian Cherokee we witness some remarkable experiments in government and the second discovery of the alphabet, accomplishments which in the first quarter of the nineteenth century exceeded the cultural attainments of the white population of the neighborhood. Classified ethnographically, the Southeast is the home of the Muskhogean tribes; Kroeber's Atlantic Coast areas, which are divided into North, Middle, and South Atlantic Slope sub-areas, comprise exclusively Algonquians in their northern and middle slopes from New Brunswick south to Virginia and North Carolina where, in the South Atlantic Slope area, the tidewater Algonquians give over the river valleys to a few Iroquoians, notably the Tuscarora and Nottoway, and the eastern Siouan tribes occupy the Piedmont. Along the Appalachian Summit we find the main body of the Iroquoians ranging from the Cherokee of the Great Smokies northward to the Seneca of western New York who with the Cayuga, Onondaga, Oneida, and Mohawk were the Five Nations of the League. These together with the other northern Iroquoian tribes, including the Huron, inhabit the Lower Great Lakes and spill over into the Ohio Valley. There we have omitted only mobile Algonquians like the Shawnee who were always on the move ahead of the frontier, and the Ottawa and Ojibwa of the Western Great Lakes (Erminie Wheeler-Voegelin, W. Vernon Kinietz, C. C. Trowbridge).

Except for the studies already mentioned, the Algonquian tribes of the Middle Slope in Maryland and Delaware have remained almost exclusively the province of amateur historians, archeologists, and ethnologists who, under the leadership of C. A. Weslager of Wilmington, have given us the best reports we have. The Wilmington group publishes in the *Bulletin of the Archaeological Society of Delaware* studies of such topics as "Indian Land Sales," "A Discussion of the Family

Hunting Territory Question in Delaware," and "Indian Tribes of the Delmarva Peninsula"; and Weslager has done two books of which *Delaware's Forgotten Folk: The Story of the Moors and Nanticokes* (1943) proves what the amateur scholar can do on problems which the professional scholar cannot afford to tackle.

The Delaware themselves have defied description. I say this in full knowledge of two classic accounts from the late eighteenth century: *An Account of the History, Manners, and Customs, of the Indian Nations, who Once Inhabited Pennsylvania and the Neighbouring States* by J. G. E. Heckewelder (1819), and the *History of Northern American Indians* written by David Zeisberger (1721-1808) and published in 1910. I might compound my error by mentioning Daniel Brinton's *The Lenape and Their Legends* (1885), which is the epic of the Walam Olum or red painted scores on which Eli Lilly has lavished a fortune. A handsome new edition of the Walam Olum has recently been prepared by the Indiana Historical Society. Both M. R. Harrington and F. G. Speck have described the ceremonies which were carried to Ontario and Oklahoma by the descendants of the Delaware. In his *King of the Delawares: Teedyuscung* (1949), Anthony F. C. Wallace relates such ethnological interests as the interplay of family band and hunting territories to a new kind of "Life and Times" account of an Indian chief whose peculiar personality, viewed through the lens of modern psychology, epitomizes Indian-white relations in eighteenth-century Pennsylvania. Dr. Wallace is currently working on a similar life of Handsome Lake, the Seneca prophet. These are all good to excellent accounts, but it was not until William W. Newcomb, Jr. published *The Culture and Acculturation of the Delaware Indians* (1956) that we got a general guide to the history and ethnology of the Delaware.

From the Delaware through the Mahican of the Hudson Valley to the Wappinger tribes of southern New England lies a natural transition area from the South Atlantic Slope to the North Atlantic Slope of northern New England. The one good guide to this whole area is Regina Flannery's *An Analysis of Coastal Algonquian Culture* (1939), which, while testing the method of cultural analysis developed by the late Professor John M. Cooper at Catholic University of America, groups the references to ethnological and historical literature of a vast area under some 327 cultural traits. The work is invaluable for comparative purposes although it makes no pretense of conveying the life of the people. Excepting perhaps Roger Williams, *A Key into the Language of America* (1643), there is no systematic account of a New England tribe south of the Merrimac. Quite good general accounts, however, commence with Gookin's *Historical Collection of the Indians in New England* . . . (1792), and in recent times C. C. Willoughby collected a series of articles on dress and ornaments, gardens, bowls, and other items of material culture in his *Antiquities of the New England Indians* (1935). F. G. Rainey made a similar but more exhaustive "Compilation of Historical Data Contributing to the Ethnography of Connecticut and Southern New England Indians" (1936) which was brought out in mimeograph form by the Archeological Society of Connecticut and is now quite rare. Speck as usual contributes first-hand ethnological studies of special topics, of which *Native Tribes and Dialects of Connecticut: A Mohegan-Pequot Diary* (1928) represents his first field work with languages and cultures now extinct, and *Territorial Subdivisions and Boundaries of the Wampanoag, Massachusetts, and Nauset Indians* (1928) reflects a preoccupation with native land tenure and a willingness to combine science, history, and folklore such as few would dare attempt.

Crossing into Maine, where the hunting culture of the Wabnaki or Northeastern Algonquians lasted considerably after white occupation of coastal towns, Speck has again given us *Penobscot Man* (1940), and Alfred G. Bailey, a historian trained under the anthropologist T. F. McIlwraith at Toronto, has related *The Conflict of European and Eastern Algonkian Cultures* (1937). Although the Wallises have recently published a general study of the Micmac Indians of Eastern Canada, which unfortunately does not distinguish historical periods, we are still largely dependent on early writers for our knowledge of the Micmac. Father Chrestien le Clercq's *New Relation of Gaspesia* (1691) belongs in this genre.

Before World War II, a group of us met to summarize what was known of the Indian cultures of northeastern North America in a symposium held at Andover, Massachusetts, in honor of Professor Speck. The Andover Symposium considered the environment, archeology, physical types, linguistic considerations, psychological characteristics, mythology, and cultures of farmers and hunters; but several of the papers were casualties of the war and were not published in *Man in Northeastern North America* (1946), which was edited by Frederick Johnson and contains an unusually valuable bibliography. Afterward I wrote a review article in the *American Anthropologist* (1948), called "The Present Status of Anthropology in Northeastern North America," summarizing the symposium. No one has yet steeled himself to going through the enormous ethnological and historical literature that exists for New England alone with a view to preparing an "Algonquians of New England"; and whoever accepts this challenge will have to face up to the archives of Massachusetts, Rhode Island, and Connecticut, and study the map collections at the John Carter Brown Library and elsewhere, for the Indian deeds of New England hold the story of land tenure and tell a good deal about tribal organization. At times it is rumored that someone has made this search, but I have not seen the results.

The people who were feared above all others by the Algonquians and Siouans alike were the Iroquois or Five Nations of New York who, to quote Cadwallader Colden, "think themselves by Nature superior to the rest of Mankind." Surpassing all others, in their own lights, they enforced the "Great Peace" by destroying everything outside the narrow limits of their confederacy, pursuing victims, it is said, to the very gates of Boston, to the banks of the Mississippi, or into the canebrakes of Georgia. Those tribes who were not destroyed were adopted or held in subjugation so that by the beginning of the eighteenth century they exacted tribute in wampum from the Delaware and New England tribes. Colden claims to have witnessed two old men going about every year or two to receive this tribute, and notes the anxiety of the Indians visited while the two old men remained in their country. It is easy to visualize "an old *Mohawk Sachem,* in a poor Blanket and a dirty Shirt . . . issuing his Orders. . . ." For Colden knew the Mohawks, and although his *History of the Five Nations* (1727) was written to stop the Indian trade with Canada, he believed in quoting from the registers, by which he meant the New York Indian Records (1678-1698). Nevertheless, his insights are remarkable even when he cribs from Father Joseph François Lafitau.

The French, who had reason to hate the Iroquois, communicated their anxiety at length in the *Jesuit Relations,* and the Jesuit fathers sent to their missions in New France men who were scholars of history, grammar, and ethnology. Almost at the end of their long regime came Lafitau (1681-1746) to live among the Mohawks at Sault St. Louis outside of Montreal where he discovered ginseng and brought the first use of the comparative method to American ethnology. His great work *Moeurs des Sauvages Ameriquains* (Paris, 1724), written after returning to France, demonstrates the first appreciation of the classificatory kinship system of the Iroquois and contains the clearest early account of political structure. Such appreciation is not manifest again for a century until Lewis Henry Morgan wrote his classic *League of the Ho-dé-no-sau-nee, or Iroquois* (1851). Since then so much ink has been spilled over the Iroquois that their combined ethnological and historical bibliography exceeds that of any primitive people. As guides to this vast literature I have used James C. Pilling, *Bibliography of the Iroquoian Languages* (1888), although it should be brought up to date; and for history, *The Wars of the Iroquois* by George T. Hunt (1940). Historians may find useful, if tortuous reading, my essay, "Problems Arising from the Historic Northeastern Position of the Iroquois" (1940). In it are the details on Iroquoian ethnic entities, and five major periods in Iroquois cultural history are offered as a frame of reference for future studies. In this paper we are concerned with the last three. The French period of wars with the Iroquois we shall pass over lightly, but the English period of the colonial wars and Indian treaties is the heart of our interest, and we stop just short of the modern Reservation period which begins with land cessions and the vision of Handsome Lake, the prophet.

We have not at present a satisfactory history of the Six Nations nor an up-to-date ethnography of the Iroquois, although various topics of the culture have been treated exhaustively by J. N. B. Hewitt, Frederick W. Waugh, Arthur C. Parker, Speck, and myself. I can point with some satisfaction, however, to two monographs which represent the living tradition in Iroquois scholarship: a *Symposium on Local Diversity in Iroquois Culture* (1951), which I edited, and Wallace's recent monograph on the Tuscarora Indians (1952). These two volumes are representative of reports in archeology, ethnology, history, and linguistics coming out of the Conference on Iroquois Research, which has met annually since 1945 at Red House, New York. It seems appropriate in this connection to acknowledge the sustained interest and support of the American Philosophical Society and of Dr. William E. Lingelbach in particular, who has kept Iroquoian studies constantly before the Library Committee of the Society.

To close this survey of ethnic entities in Eastern America and to end the census of ethnological models, I mention several general bibliographies. George P. Murdock has twice compiled a comprehensive *Ethnographic Bibliography of North America* (1941, 2d edn., 1953), classified by culture areas and tribal entities; and for our purposes, I recommend Irving Rouse and John M. Goggin, *An Anthropological Bibliography of the Eastern Seaboard* (1947), since it also contains local history. Northeastern scholars depend on McIlwraith's annual list of publications in ethnology, anthropology, and archeology, which has run since 1925 in the *Canadian Historical Review* (Toronto).

Before turning to the literature of the council fire some explanation of how the ethnographer classifies cultures seems in order. Since the culture or way of life of a society has its own unique character, it has become a maxim in ethnology that cultures should be described in terms of themselves. Finding the points of organization within a culture is difficult enough where field work is possible among the living people, but defining the major themes and constructing the patterns of a culture present an even greater problem, as every historian knows, when the society he is studying precedes his own by two centuries. The record for preliterate societies and cultures is sufficiently broad to enable the ethnologist to make cross-cultural generalizations about the content of a culture. At least we know what are the categories. Improving on Wissler's universal culture pattern, Murdock and the Yale school of ethnographers have evolved an elaborate *Outline of Cultural Materials* (1938, 1950). Their original fifty-five major categories, ranging from basic data to death, have now been expanded to eighty-eight to comprise the complexities of modern industrial societies. But such an organization is far too complex for the simple hunters and fishers and hoers of corn who peopled our Eastern Woodlands three centuries ago. Of perhaps greater interest to the historian of America is the sequence which Julian H. Steward adopted for presentation of materials in his *Handbook of South American Indians,* 6 vols. (1946-1953). It runs: introduction, tribal divisions and history, subsistence activities, villages and houses, dress and ornaments, transportation, manufactures, trade or economic organization, social and political organization, the life cycle, games and music, religion, mythology, folklore, and finally, lore and learning. This classification is a fair model of what to expect in ethnographical literature, and it has the virtue of being capable of contraction or infinite expansion.

The whole problem of the processing of anthropological materials, which all of us have to face, has been met ingeniously by the Yale group under Murdock, who discusses the evolution of the Human Relations Area Files in *Anthropology Today* (A. L. Kroeber, and others, 1953). The trouble with all such systems, however, is that the ethos of the culture escapes through the mesh. The major themes of Iroquois life are better seen through such phrases as "they are as sisters—the earth, the women, and our life sustainers (corn, beans, and squash)." Or, after Weiser's celebrated letter to Thomas Lee of Virginia, "a man is resolute, he speaks the truth, he gives the best that he has, and never shows weakness." And "the world on the turtle's back" gives us a graphic understanding of Iroquois cosmogony.

The analysis of culture into its constituent elements or traits has a certain utility, moreover, because these traits cluster in complexes which are the situational effects of major cultural activities; and the traits, complexes, and activities move about on the map as customs are diffused from people to people, sometimes losing their original consistency and appearing elsewhere in otherwise quite different wholes. Thus the principal traits associated with maize culture have been diffused everywhere that corn will grow throughout the Eastern Woodlands. Maize culture everywhere permits semisedentary village life, frees the village elders from hunting to attend council and develop political forms, and, where corn yields a surplus, a well-developed cycle of first-fruits ceremonies divides the year between a winter festival and the green corn busk. We would expect the Eastern Siouans, who were primarily hunters, to offer less resistance to white encroachment on their lands than the more sedentary Cherokee, Five Nations, or Creek Confederacy. Comparative studies of American tribal organization show a correlation between type of social structure and cultural stability. The tradition of the League keeps the Iroquois who live on the Six Nations Reserve in Canada politically active today whereas the Tutelo of Virginia, who took refuge among the Cayuga in the mid-eighteenth century, are extinct.

It is, furthermore, possible to classify cultures in terms of their major concerns or interests, to which Herskovits has given the name "cultural focus." One might say that the principal concerns of Iroquois life were kinship, the maize complex, hunting, going on the warpath, holding councils, attending treaties, and death. The theme of death runs through the treaty literature. Its manifestation is the condolence ceremony, through which the people continually requickened life itself. The ceremony centers about the Six Songs of farewell to the dead chief, one for each rank of society, in which the matrons who represent the life of the tribe link the warriors and the deceased founders of the League. The League, of course, was the climax form of Iroquois social structure of which the maternal household was the core image. In the Iroquois joint-family longhouse there developed a pattern of social life, with the two halves of the family living across the fire, which became the symbol of a society. When enlarged by projection from village to tribe to confederacy, the Longhouse of the League with its central fire was to dominate Indian-white relations throughout the colonies.

III

The literature of the council fire is vast indeed. For every bundle of sticks, wampum belt or string, and painted score by which Indian wampum keepers recalled the promises of the whites and kept a record of relations with surrounding tribes, the white man wrote down things for us to read many generations later. The proceedings of treaties held with the Indians were written into journals and incorporated as minutes of the provincial councils. Indian commissioners appointed by the several colonies maintained "Indian Records" of talks with visiting chiefs and agenda of items to be taken up at later councils. Above all the Indian commissioners sent back through official channels detailed accounts of their activities and negotiations. While much of such material still exists in manuscript form and is preserved in archives in this country and in Europe, a good deal of it got into print beginning with the publication by Henry De Puy of *A Bibliography of the English Colonial Treaties with the Indians* (1917). And thanks to Carl Van Doren and Julian P. Boyd we have a tall book of *Indian Treaties Printed by Benjamin Franklin, 1736-1762* (1938). Van Doren's crisp introduction properly ascribes the Condoling Ceremony to the Iroquois, and to Franklin the realization that in treaty literature he had a publisher's first, while Boyd has contributed the most considerable essay on Pennsylvania Indian affairs.

Printed sources abound. The *New York Colonial Documents,* Peter Wraxall's *Abridgement of the Indian Affairs . . . in the Colony of New York,* the *Livingston Indian Records,* and the *Sir William Johnson Papers* carry the affairs of the Six Nations to the Revolution. The *Pennsylvania Colonial Records* and the *Pennsylvania Archives* support these and tell the story of the Delaware and Shawnee. The *Maryland Archives* provide abundant information concerning the Indians with whom Lord Baltimore's colony had dealings, while Swem's *Virginia Historical Index* yields a rich harvest of references not only to the tribes tributary to Virginia, but to Indians such as the Iroquois, Tuscarora, and Cherokee whose activities also affected the colony.

In three recent papers I have listed manuscript collections bearing on the political history of the Six Nations, and since I am preparing with George Snyderman a more comprehensive list, be it said here that there exists an unworked mine of historical manuscripts bearing on Indian affairs in the early national period. For example, the papers of Samuel Kirkland (Hamilton College Library), Henry Knox and Timothy Pickering (Massachusetts Historical Society), and Israel Chapin, father and son (New-York Historical Society) contain much information. Snyderman, working in Philadelphia repositories, found rich store in the Quaker Records; and Paul A. W. Wallace has recently described the Moravian Records. It is pleasant indeed to find the collections of the British Museum and other English repositories so adequately represented by photostats and microfilm at the Library of Congress.

In this search I have continually come upon the traces of other scholars. To make an *ad hoc* classification of the topics to which historians have addressed themselves, I have put down Indian Wars, Trade, Treaties and Laws, Land Cessions, Captivities, Lives of Indians and Lives of Indian Agents, and Folklore. Samuel Penhallow, William Hubbard, Samuel Drake, and Herbert Sylvester, beginning in 1726, have written of the history of the wars of New England. There are at least three modern studies of the *Wars of the Iroquois:* the volume by

George T. Hunt with this title (1940), already mentioned, Snyderman, *Behind the Tree of Peace* (1948), and Raymond Scheele, *Warfare of the Iroquois and Their Northern Neighbors* (1950). Hunt, a trained historian, brought a rigorous discipline to Indian historiography, but his book shows little appreciation of the culture of the people. Snydermaɪ and Scheele are anthropologists trained in history. Hunt followed Charles H. McIlwain who first demonstrated the importance of the fur trade in securing the continuous alliance of the Six Nations to the Dutch and British interest. The chain of friendship that stretched from Onondaga to Albany was fully appreciated by Governor Thomas Dongan of New York and by James Logan in Philadelphia, and as fully deplored by the Marquis de Denonville in Canada. Securing the friendship of the Six Nations became the firm policy of the King's ministers at Whitehall; to break up the Longhouse was the fixed intention of the French.

Despite efforts among historians to bridge the gap between documentary history and ethnology no one has yet succeeded in producing a book which is securely footed in both disciplines. Randolph Downes very nearly maintained the "Indian point of view" in *Council Fires on the Upper Ohio* (1940). Wilbur Jacobs, writing primarily from historical sources, was not completely convincing in his attempt to prove Indian gifts a major motivating force in the westward movement. The fault lies partly in the sources themselves. Virtually all that we know of Indians at the time comes to us through the eyes and pens of white men whose interests and values differed from those of the Indians. How different from our own were the basic "Concepts of Land Ownership among the Iroquois and Their Neighbors" (Snyderman, 1951) that land could neither be bartered nor sold! Even the Johnsons—Sir William, Guy, and Sir John—James Logan, Samuel Kirkland, Philip Schuyler, Timothy Pickering, and Witham Marshe, to whom we owe the records of Indian and white negotiations, were the products of colonial society and brought the biases of that society to their observations. The Iroquois sensed this in their remarks about Conrad Weiser, the celebrated Pennsylvania interpreter, whom they recognized as a cultural hybrid: "He is of our Nation, and a Member of our Council as well as yours. When we adopted him we divided him into Two equal Parts. . . ."

The question of land lay behind the laws and treaties in which the whites engaged the Indians. Clarence W. Alvord and Helen Shaw have treated the development of British policy in this regard; and Charles C. Royce and Cyrus Thomas have codified land cessions and treaties; and the supporting collections to *American State Papers—Indian Affairs* (1832-1834) are covered in Mohr's *Federal Indian Relations, 1774-1788* (1933). Curiously, it is in a popular book that D'Arcy McNickle, himself an Indian and formerly an official in the Bureau of Indian Affairs, sees the broad sweep of a developing national Indian policy, and he has pointed up significant problems on which historical research is needed. He has foreseen the need to assess the contributions of the Six Nations to the political thinking of the founding fathers, a topic which has attracted Van Doren and Boyd, and he wonders why the public career of Henry Knox has escaped a biographer. Timothy Pickering, who, as Knox's deputy, was first Commissioner of Indian Affairs in the federal government, has attracted more attention.

Narratives of Indian captivities have long been the domain of the collector but more recently it has attracted the bibliographer. R. G. W. Vail's useful guide, *The Voice of the Old Frontier* (1949), has opened the whole field to study. Before this bibliography appeared researchers relied on the list of the magnificent Ayer Collection at the Newberry Library. Vail was the first scholar to have access to the captivities collection of the late Frank C. Deering of Saco, Maine. Marius Barbeau has made a more recent study of this collection as a part of a larger bibliographical project. The National Museum of Canada will soon publish his 1,700 page analytical catalog of all the important collections of captivity narratives, which will put the knowledge of these rarities in the hands of everyone. Barbeau has already published a description of the notable collection of Mrs. Arthur M. Greenwood (American Philosophical Society, *Proceedings*, 94 (1950), 526).

Captivity literature has long appealed to the literary scholar for its exotic flavor, but not until recently has it attracted the ethnologist or the historian. Swanton, as usual, pointed the way in a brief paper on the conflict of cultures ("Notes on the Mental Assimilation of Races"), in which he observed that the whites quite often preferred Indian society to the restraints of colonial society; his paper, however, has escaped notice. More recently Roy Harvey Pearce has seen the captivity narrative as illustrating the "horror" component of the "savagism" of the American Indian.

Indian captivity narratives, the lives of Indian chiefs, and the careers of the great Indian agents and interpreters form a field for the historical biographer. I suppose that Howard Peckham (*Pontiac,* 1947) and the Wallaces, Paul A. W. and Anthony F. C., father and son, are the heirs of the "Life and Times" tradition of Samuel G. Drake and William L. Stone. Drake badly needs a bibliographer, and Brant and Red Jacket as persons somehow eluded Stone. Peckham had considerable help from Kinietz on the Ottawa, and his historical research leaves little to be desired, although few can touch the noble style of Francis Parkman. Paul Wallace's life of *Conrad Weiser* (1945) is one of the most readable and valuable source books on the Six Nations. There are materials for a similar life of Samuel Kirkland. Is Sir William Johnson too well known?

IV

If history and ethnology have a common area of interest in Indian and white relations, is there a body of theory or a method for combining the two approaches? As Alfred L. Kroeber has written, "without culture patterns, culture elements, culture changes and processes, we [ethnologists] would have little else left to us" that is not preempted elsewhere. On the other hand there is history, and there is historiography, which I take to be the critical and constructive process by which history is written. All of us who have worked in the two fields I have just reviewed have perforce become historians, but the method which has developed in ethnological and archeological studies in this country has been called the "direct historic approach" and of late "ethno-history." That the two disciplines are integrated by more than the hyphen in the word I will attempt to show presently. If the implied combination is to be fruitful, the first desideratum is a long, documented record of the past—a span of dated human history. Such is assured. Next comes an extensive ethnographic and historical literature, which we also have. Third there is a need for scholars trained in either history or ethnology and, above all, for persons possessing both competences. The latter should be the first item on our agenda of common tasks.

What then are the aims and purposes of ethnohistorical study? They seem to be four-fold. The primary aim has been to use the ethnological present to throw light on the archeological past. This first use of ethnohistory for reconstruction has been called the "direct historic approach" and was first used extensively by the archeologists William Duncan Strong and Waldo Rudolph Wedel who found that by working backwards from known historic sites they could identify others in the protohistoric past. Here the method runs out and other methods come into play. Carl E. Guthe claims that ethnohistorical studies developed simultaneously in 1934 at the University of Chicago and at the University of Michigan; but such arguments are specious, for Nels Christian Nelson developed the method in the Southwest twenty years before that, and Swanton used his own field work for interpreting historic documents for many years. Recently Fred Eggan has discussed some of the implications of the method for linking "Ethnological Cultures and Their Archeological Backgrounds" in all of Eastern North America. Research of this kind, he points out, "is so specialized and time-consuming that its activities need to be coordinated and centralized." Whether such a center should be at an academic institution or receive government support he does not say. But he goes so far as to venture that we know enough about social structures and how a limited number of forms relate to various economic and environmental factors to reconstruct a good deal besides prehistoric material cultures. The direct historic approach then has come a long way, but it continues to be concerned with ethnic entities: their identification, location, contacts, movements, and relationships to neighboring groups.

Second, ethnohistory may elucidate later historical problems. Indian tribal names, personal names, and place names plague the colonial historian. Only the ethnologist who is trained in linguistics and has some experience in the particular language family can help the historian. Confronted by a list of chiefs who signed a certain agreement the historian can compare other neighboring documents to see where else the names appear. But he cannot find out, without having studied the social system of the tribe in question and its naming customs, which names are merely titles that will be carried again and again by different individuals from generation to generation, as for example the Mohawk title *Tekarihoken* or their name for the Governor of Virginia, *Asarekowah*. Place names lead from linguistics to the treacherous morass of cartography which is the historian's province. The point is that the ethnologist can frequently tell the historian how discrete items relate to other wholes. The colonial historian may be concerned with certain unique events at certain times and places, such as the Lancaster Treaty of 1744, the Albany Congress of 1754, and the Treaty at Buffalo Creek in 1838. At all of these gatherings the Six Nations insisted on performing the rite of condolence before any business was transacted. Analyzing the proceedings into constituent parts, the ethnologist recognizes a repeated pattern of sequence, and nothing unique.

Third, as scientists we recognize the potential contribution that ethnohistory may make to cultural theory. The direct historic approach has given us considerable insight into cultural process. We gain access to the problems of cultural stability and cultural change by utilizing the dated record to measure duration of conservatism and to detect innovations. Ethnologists have shied away from this approach.

Finally, there are certain implications for linguistics that pertain to the direct historic approach and to later history. Language remains one of the best tools for historical reconstruction because of its essential conservatism and our knowledge of the process of linguistic change. As the work of Benjamin Lee Whorf and George L. Trager on Uto-Aztecan may solve the riddle of Southwestern archeology by linking certain archeological manifestations to the ancestors of present tribal societies, so Morris Swadesh has recently developed a quantitative method for testing linguistic borrowing and determining genetic relationships. Libraries contain early grammars and vocabularies of Indian languages and some of these languages are still spoken and can be studied by modern methods. It should be possible to determine rates of change, measure dialectical differentiation, and test mutual intelligibility. The realities of cultural process can then be projected backwards. The chances of rapid progress in this direction seem remote just now because the number of linguists is small.

To conclude the discussion of how methods of ethnology combine with historiography in the practice of ethnohistory, may I say that what ethnology contributes to ethnohistorical study is a point of view and method which I have called "upstreaming." If I may paraphrase myself, application of the viewpoint rests on three assumptions: 1) that major patterns of culture remain stable over long periods of time, producing repeated uniformities; 2) these patterns can best be seen by proceeding from the known ethnological present to the unknown past, using recent sources first and then earlier sources; 3) those sources which ring true at both ends of the time span merit confidence. Although effective, this method must be used with caution because it contains a built-in fallacy which historians will recognize as the doctrine of uniformitarianism, which infers past from present. The ethnohistorian threads a narrow course between the rock of assumed stability and the morass of assumed acculturation. Margaret T. Hodgen has contributed significantly to the resolution of this dilemma in a recent application of ethnological methods to dated history of innovation in Britain (*Change and History,* 1952).

V

We have just walked where the earth is narrow near the bog of theory. Let us now return to the clearing at the woods' edge where we kindled a small fire, and there we will sit down across the fire and share a pipe and condole one another with words of kindness. So far we have been careful not to throw ashes in each other's eyes. Of such was the drama of forest diplomacy, which might be entitled "Condolence and Calumet," a play that derived from an Iroquois ceremony and in which the actors were Indian sachems and colonial governors. With different casts and slight changes in the script it ran for over a century, principally at Albany, but occasionally at Philadelphia, Lancaster, Easton, Johnson Hall, Ft. Stanwix, and Canandaigua. Sometimes there were French actors when the play was staged at Montreal. But in its purest form it was performed at the great drama festivals held each fall at Onondaga where it is said the ceremony originated with the founding of the League of the Five Nations before the Dutch came to America. Deganawidah was its author and Hiawatha its leading actor, according to *The Iroquois Book of Rites* (Horatio Hale, 1883; see also Paul Wallace's *The White Roots of Peace,* 1946). That the reader may judge how much of this ceremony is still carried in the cultural memories of the Six Nations today I have described "An Iroquois Condolence Council for Installing Cayuga Chiefs in 1945," which I was privileged to witness. Since the *Journal of the Washington Academy of Sciences* has recently been indexed, but may not be accessible, I mention *The Roll Call of the Iroquois Chiefs* . . . (Smithsonian *Misc. Coll.,* 1950), a study of a mnemonic cane by which the old men preserved the order of the founders and kept an organization chart of their government.

Though the cane itself dated from the nineteenth century, the mnemonic is as old as the ceremony.

The program of the Condolence Council comprises some sixteen events which are arranged in a pattern of sequence that has evidently governed its performance since early times. The pattern can best be understood if it is remembered that one side, called the Clearminded, condole or perform the ceremony to lift up the minds of the Mourners who have recently lost a chief.

Program of the Condolence Council for the Installation of Chiefs among the Six Nations

1. Procession: taking the ceremony over the path to the house of the Mourners, calling out the roll of the Founders on the way (Clearminded).

2. Welcome at the fire by the woods (Mourners).

3. The three bare words of requickening: tears, ears, and throat (Both sides).

4. Taking them by the arm to the council place (Mourners).

5. The Roll Call or Eulogy, called "Putting their house in order" (Clearminded).

6. Farewell chant to the Dead Chief: the Six Songs (less one). (Clearminded behind a blanket).

7. Over the Great Forest (Part one): recitation of the laws (Clearminded).

8. The Sixth Song to the Founders (Clearminded partitioned).

9. Over the Forest (Part two).

10. The balance of the Requickening Address with wampum strings: the Clearminded threaten to withdraw but are asked to stay until the Mourners can compose a reply.

11. The Six Songs: the reply of the Mourners (Mourners).

12. Condolences and wampums returned (Mourners).

13. Showing the face of the new chief (Mourners).

14. Charge to the new chief and to the public (Clearminded).

15. The Feast to wash away the tobacco. *Yohee Hii yah.*

16. Rubbing Antlers: the dance of celebration, in which the hosts release their women folk to the other party and society is restored.

Fulfillment of the rite illustrates certain principles which are implicit in the pattern of sequence and are consequences of one half of the society condoling the other half whose minds are down with grief. Note separation or withdrawal on death; messages go both ways and a procession nears the fire of the mourners; there we witness alternation, then self-reciprocation as parts of the Six Songs and recitation of the laws are separated and interdigitated; and then the side which has spoken offers to withdraw politely and give the other side time to compose a reply, but they remain on appeal and avoid an affront. Then comes the reply to all that has been said, followed by the climax when the chiefship is restored, after which the reunion of society is accomplished in the dance. From the death of the chief to the post-climactic social dance society goes the full cycle from dysphoria to euphoria. Thus by fulfilling the functional theory of Radcliffe-Brown, in illustrating Malinowski's concept of reciprocity, and in representing to the Iroquois a point of cultural intensity, the Condolence Council becomes something of an ethnological showpiece.

But the condoling ceremony also has long cultural roots. All of the principles just mentioned and nearly every one of the items listed above occur in the proceedings of conferences held between Indians and whites. By eliminating repetitions in the elaborate program, the items may be reduced to ten and the principles to about four. We cannot expect to find all of the items listed in all of the treaty proceedings, for observers described what they knew, and there were few initiates like Asher Wright, Conrad Weiser, Guy Johnson, and Robert Livingston who understood the language and had seen the ceremony more than once. The traits appear under different names—such as Road, Fire, Chain, and Presents—as earlier writers denote aspects of an activity which struck them. Still other features are no longer present. An analysis of all of the occasions for which there are records from the most recent to the earliest would, I believe, show a remarkable continuity of its major features.

VI

What now are the common tasks which history and ethnology can undertake for the common enrichment of both disciplines?

1. Conferences of historians and ethnologists, beginning with the Newberry Library Conference on Indian Studies held in March of 1952,

afford a means of getting together on common ground to discuss materials and methods of history and cultural studies. They may give rise to unexpected but welcome results. The Conference on Indian Studies led indirectly to the Carnegie Corporation's joint grant to the University of Chicago, the Newberry Library, and the Chicago Natural History Museum for the study of certain problems relating to the Philippine Islands, specifically for the appointment of two fellows to work in the Ayer Collection, calendaring the Philippine manuscripts and preparing a monograph on mission history. A more direct result was a conference of local historians, archeologists, and ethnologists working on Indian claims cases, held at Columbus, Ohio, in 1952, which characteristically formed a new society for ethnohistorical study. A third result is the present lecture.

If, however, ethnohistory is to develop as a field of study, historians and ethnologists should probably first meet in the focus of a common research problem. Areas of agreement and disagreement might then be aired at symposia during professional meetings of the two groups.

Mature scholars, who have participated in joint research efforts, may want to offer seminars in departments of history and anthropology which will attract and train a new kind of student. Historians who have shared research with ethnologists may find themselves training young anthropologists, and some history majors will be learning historiography from ethnohistorians. The question may then arise, what to call the anthropologist trained by an historian, to distinguish him from the historian trained by an ethnologist. Such problems will probably be settled by the individual who decides where his kudos lies, just as we anthropologists take on protective coloration when we find ourselves among natural and physical scientists at the National Research Council, perchance among social scientists at the Social Science Research Council, or sharing ideas with humanists at the American Council of Learned Societies.

2. The summer seminar or work conference has enjoyed considerable success in the sciences when some new development is about to break. Bringing the thinking workers together for a season will sometimes spark the desired reaction. The Social Science Research Council has used this model repeatedly and might be encouraged to facilitate the assembling of a small study group of historians and anthropologists to

explore the common ground between the disciplines. The group might meet near a large research library, as is the custom among historians during their vacations from teaching. In this setting the anthropologists would be the principal beneficiaries, since the historians would be working in their own element. But I suspect that the historians might profit by forgoing books and manuscripts and gathering in a location where experienced field workers could help them observe and participate in the oral tradition. Santa Fe, with its laboratories, museums and libraries in close proximity to the Rio Grande Pueblos, offers something of both and might be an ideal location. My own experience argues for holding field and library as mutually exclusive variables which are best worked in alternation.

3. A central register of documents relating to Indian and white relations emerges as one of the needs of lawyers, historians, and anthropologists who are currently researching Indian claims. The National Archives in Washington remains the largest single repository of materials bearing on Federal-Indian relations, but a vast deal of manuscript material is scattered in local repositories, and its total range and content are probably unknown to any single person. Much of the research on Indian claims is going on outside of Washington, moreover, wherever there are universities with departments of anthropology or history given to this specialty. Either the researcher comes to Washington to work with the originals or takes them home in photo-copy. No one knows what any other person has seen. When all of the cases are prepared and filed and the courts have settled the claims, there will have been great duplication of effort and probably significant gaps will remain in the record. Good and bad historical study is being paid for at rates which competent historians can seldom command. We owe it to history, to the Indians, and to ourselves as taxpayers to improve the quality of the effort.

4. An institute for American Indian history and culture has sometimes been rumored and one day may be expected to arise from the smoke of prairie fires. What would be more appropriate than an L. H. Morgan chair in American ethnology, or a Sequoia Press for American Indian languages? Can we not form a new conspiracy to promote a Pontiac lectureship in American Indian history?

5. Support is never beyond reach when good projects are in the

offing. Projects may need rephrasing, though, to conform with the current jargon of foundations and to fit the fashion of the moment. Without rewording or alteration, I will list but four tasks which need doing and probably will get done when some bright graduate student finds a researchable problem which one or another of them illustrates. The story of the supplanting of the Indian in New England has not been done in style since Gookin's day. The role of the Six Nations in the foundation of the Republic is a task which I hope one day to discharge. And I cannot fathom why the abundant materials for historical biographies of Knox, Pickering, and Kirkland have been by-passed so long by historians. To be certain, Kirkland presents special aspects, being at once missionary, ethnologist, educator, and patriot, but perhaps he gives us the focus we have been looking for to get started.

Indian and White Relations in Eastern North America:
A Common Ground for History and Ethnology

Bibliography

BY LYMAN H. BUTTERFIELD, WILCOMB E. WASHBURN,
AND WILLIAM N. FENTON

PART I

REFERENCE AND BIBLIOGRAPHICAL AIDS

The present bibliography, as stated in the Foreword, is selective. The student should not, however, overlook the standard national bibliographies such as Joseph Sabin, *Bibliotheca Americana: A Dictionary of Books Relating to America from its Discovery to the Present Time,* begun by Joseph Sabin, continued by Wilberforce Eames, and completed by R. W. G. Vail (N. Y., 1868-1936), 29 vols.; and Charles Evans, *American Bibliography: A Chronological Dictionary of All Books, Pamphlets, and Periodical Publications Printed in the United States of America from the Genesis of Printing in 1639 down to and Including the Year 1800* (Chicago and Worcester, Mass., 1903-1955), 13 vols., the last volume of which was edited by Clifford K. Shipton. The student should also consult Henry P. Beers, comp., *Bibliographies in American History* (N. Y., 1938), J. N. Larned, ed., *The Literature of American History: A Bibliographical Guide* (Boston, 1902; repr. Columbus, O., 1953), and other predecessors of the *Harvard Guide to American History* which are discussed below. The "Critical Essays on Authorities" in the first five volumes of the *History of American Life* series, edited by Dixon Ryan Fox and Arthur M. Schlesinger (N. Y., 1927-1944), contain specialized bibliographies. A helpful tool for finding articles published in the nineteenth century is William Frederick Poole, and others, *Poole's Index to Periodical Literature, 1802-1906,* rev. edn. and supplements (Boston, 1882-1908; repr. N. Y., 1938). For literature in the twentieth

century check the *Reader's Guide to Periodical Literature* (N. Y., 1900-
). The student should also be acquainted with the *Bibliographic
Index: A Cumulative Bibliography of Bibliographies* (N. Y., 1937-   )
which lists *all* works containing bibliographies.

Clark, Thomas D., ed., *Travels in the Old South; a Bibliography*
(Norman, Okla., 1956). 2 vols., 330, 292 p.

Vols. I-II, covering the years 1527-1825, contain travel accounts
and geographical descriptions concerning the southern colonies and
states, with a summary of content and critical comments on each
item. Numerous references to Indian life and customs.

Comas, Juan, *Bibliografía Selectiva de las Culturas Indígenas de
América* (Mexico City, 1953). 292 p., maps.

Publication No. 166 of the Comisión de Historia of the Instituto
Panamericano de Geografía e Historia.

Davis, Eliza Jeffries, and E. G. R. Taylor, comps., *Guide to Periodicals
and Bibliographies Dealing with Geography, Archaeology, and
History,* Historical Association Pamphlet No. 110 (London, 1938).
22 p.

De Puy, Henry F., comp., *A Bibliography of the English Colonial
Treaties with the American Indians, including a Synopsis of Each
Treaty* (N. Y., 1917). Unpaged, facsims.

Includes 50 facsimile titles of printed treaties, 1677-1769, with
bibliographical and historical notes on the treaties.

"Dissertations in Anthropology: Submitted to Educational Institutions
of the World in Partial Fulfillment of Requirements of the Ph.D.
Degree or Equivalent," *Yearbook of Anthropology,* Vol. I (N. Y.:
Wenner-Gren Foundation for Anthropological Research, 1955),
701-752.

Dockstader, Frederick J., comp., *Graduate Studies on the American
Indian: A Bibliography of Theses and Dissertations,* Mus. Amer.
Indian, Heye Foundation, *Contributions,* 15 (N. Y., [1957?]).
Approx. 400 p.

This forthcoming bibliography of theses is a "must" for the
graduate student selecting a dissertation topic in the field. The sub-
title of the volume is "A bibliography of theses and dissertations
from colleges and universities in the United States, Canada, and

Mexico," and the compiler believes that it includes 90% of all theses which deal in any way with the Indian. The term Indian is defined to include aborigines of North, Central, and South America, plus the Eskimo. The bibliography is not confined to anthropological theses, but includes dissertations in history, sociology, art, education, and other non-ethnological fields. The data was obtained from 186 schools; 148 more were checked but lacked any "Indian" theses. The bibliography will include about 3,500 entries, many annotated, and the whole indexed by tribe and by subject.

Doctoral Dissertations Accepted by American Universities. Compiled for the Association of Research Libraries, 1933 to date, by various editors, and published by the H. W. Wilson Company, New York.

Douglas, Frederick H., comp., *A Guide to Articles on the American Indians in Serial Publications,* Vol. I (Denver: Denver Art Museum, 1934). 352 p., mimeographed.

Edward Eberstadt & Sons, *Indian Captivities & Massacres: Being the Contemporary Record of Caucasian Contact and Conflict with the Native American* (N. Y., [1943]). 70 p., facsims.

An example of the scholarly value of book dealers' catalogues when carefully prepared. Other dealers who occasionally issue catalogues devoted to Indians include Argosy Book Stores, N. Y. City; W. G. Tilton, Topeka, Kan.; and Charley G. Drake, Union City, Ga.

Edwards, Everett Eugene, and Wayne D. Rasmussen, *A Bibliography on the Agriculture of the American Indians* (Wash., 1942). 107 p.

Field, Thomas W., *An Essay towards an Indian Bibliography. Being a Catalogue of Books, Relating to the History, Antiquities, Languages, Customs, Religion, Wars, Literature, and Origin of the American Indians, in the Library of Thomas W. Field. With Bibliographical and Historical Notes* ... (N. Y., 1873). 430 p.

Reprinted by offset, Columbus, O., 1951. Catalogue of a notable private collection (1708 entries) later sold at auction. The annotations are still very useful, often providing virtual synopses of the works listed.

Gomme, George Laurence, *Index of Archaeological Papers, 1665-1890* (London, 1907). 910 p.

Griffin, Appleton P. C., *Bibliography of American Historical Societies*

(The United States and the Dominion of Canada), Amer. Hist. Assoc., *Ann. Report,* 1905, II (Wash., 1907). 1374 p.

Standard guide to the contents of the thousands of volumes published by national, state, and local historical societies through the year 1905. The index contains 5 columns of entries relating to Indians.

Hargrett, Lester, *A Bibliography of the Constitutions and Laws of the American Indians* (Cambridge, Mass., 1947). 124 p., facsims.

Harvard Guide to American History, ed. Oscar Handlin, Arthur Meier Schlesinger, Samuel Eliot Morison, Frederick Merk, Arthur Meier Schlesinger, Jr., and Paul Herman Buck (Cambridge, Mass., 1954). 689 p.

Successor to the *Guide to the Study and Teaching of American History,* ed. Edward Channing, Albert Bushnell Hart, and Frederick Jackson Turner (Boston, 1912). The indispensable handbook for the graduate student in American history.

Haywood, Charles, *A Bibliography of North American Folklore and Folksongs* (N. Y., 1951). 1292 p.

Book Two: "The American Indians North of Mexico," pp. 749-1159. Concentrates on folklore, beliefs, and customs, but includes extremely detailed listings of general studies both of particular tribes and of Indians in general.

Hodge, Frederick Webb, ed., *Handbook of American Indians North of Mexico,* Bur. Amer. Ethnol., *Bull.* 30, pts. 1-2 (Wash., 1907-1910; repr. 1912). 972, 1221 p., map, illus., bibliog.

Encyclopedic; long the standard reference work on Indians in the U. S. and Canada. The individual articles contain exhaustive reference notes, and the bibliography covers pp. 1179-1221 in pt. 2.

Hodgen, Margaret T., *Change and History: A Study of the Dated Distributions of Technological Innovations in England,* Wenner-Gren Foundation for Anthropol. Research, Viking Fund *Pubns. in Anthropol.,* No. 18 (N. Y., 1952). 324 p., maps, bibliog.

Index to Early American Periodicals, 1728-1860.

In New York University Library, Washington Square, N. Y. Contains four regular-sized cabinet trays filled with references to articles appearing in early American periodicals on "Indians of North America." An invaluable aid to the researcher. The index is not readily accessible to researchers and advance notice should be given before coming to New York to use the file. Slips for entries under "Indians of North America," copied for Roy Harvey Pearce, for work on his *Savages of America,* have been deposited in the Ayer Collection of the Newberry Library, Chicago. The scope and resources of the Index are described in "Index to Early American Periodical Literature, 1728-1870" (N. Y., 1941), reprinted from *Pamphleteer Monthly,* 1 (1940), Nos. 7-8. There is a project underway to microprint this Periodical Index.

Jones, John Alan, comp., *List of Unpublished Doctoral Dissertations and Masters Theses in the Field of Anthropology Bearing on North American Indians North of Mexico* (Wash.: Dept. of Justice, [1953]). 19 p., mimeographed.

Leary, Lewis, *Articles on American Literature, 1900-1950* (Durham, N. C., 1954). 437 p.
　　Section on Indians, pp. 367-368.

List of Doctoral Dissertations in History Now in Progress at Colleges and Universities in the United States, October, 1955 (Wash.: American Historical Association, [1955]). 59 p.

McCoy, James C., *Jesuit Relations of Canada, 1623-1673: A Bibliography.* Intro. by Lawrence C. Wroth (Paris, 1937). 310 p., facsims.

McIlwraith, T. F., comp., "Ethnology, Anthropology, and Archaeology" [an annual bibliographical listing contributed to "Recent Publications Relating to Canada"], *Canadian Hist. Rev.,* 6 (1925)—to date.
　　Items in other sections of this important bibliography relating to Canada are of course often pertinent.

Matthews, William, and Roy Harvey Pearce, *American Diaries: An Annotated Bibliography of American Diaries Written Prior to the Year 1861* (Berkeley, 1945). 383 p.
　　Lacks subject index, but diaries with Indian material so described in annotations.

Murdock, George Peter, *Ethnographic Bibliography of North America,* Yale Univ., *Anthropological Stud.,* 1 (New Haven, 1941), 168 p.; (2d edn., New Haven, 1953). 239 p., map.

Newberry Library, *A Bibliographical Checklist of North and Middle American Indian Linguistics in the Edward E. Ayer Collection,* comp. by Ruth Lapham Butler (Chicago, 1941). 2 vols., unpaged.

Material on 328 separate dialects or sub-dialects arranged alphabetically, with an index of authors and subjects.

Newberry Library, *Narratives of Captivity among the Indians of North America: A List of Books and Manuscripts on This Subject in the Edward E. Ayer Collection of the Newberry Library* (Chicago, 1912), 120 p.; *Supplement I* (Chicago, 1928). 49 p.

Palfrey, Thomas R., and Henry E. Coleman, Jr., comp., *Guide to Bibliographies of Theses, United States and Canada* (2d edn., Chicago, 1940). 54 p.

Pennsylvania Historical Association, *Writings on Pennsylvania History: A Bibliography* (Harrisburg, 1946). 565 p.

A *Bibliography of Pennsylvania History*, compiled by Norman B. Wilkinson, a revised and enlarged edition of *Writings on Pennsylvania History*, is currently in press.

Pierce, Roy G., comp., *Preliminary Bibliographical List of Articles, Books and References to Virginia Indians, with Particular Emphasis on Archeology* ([Richmond?] 1944). 9 p., mimeographed. Also *Bibliographical List No. 2-5* (1945-1953). 8, 13, 12, 12 p., respectively; mimeographed.

An attempt at a comprehensive listing by the librarian of the Archeological Society of Virginia; locates copies in Virginia libraries.

Pilling, James Constantine, *Bibliography of the Algonquian Languages,* Bur. Amer. Ethnol., *Bull.* 13 (Wash., 1891). 614 p., facsims.

The value of this bibliography, like all those compiled by Pilling, extends far beyond the field of linguistics.

Pilling, James Constantine, *Bibliography of the Iroquoian Languages,* Bur. Amer. Ethnol., *Bull.* 6 (Wash., 1888). 208 p., facsims.

Pilling, James Constantine, *Proof-Sheets of a Bibliography of the Languages of the North American Indians,* Bur. Amer. Ethnol., *Misc. Pubn.* 2 (Wash., 1885). 1135 p., facsims.

110 copies were printed for distribution to collaborators.

Rouse, Irving, and John M. Goggin, eds., *An Anthropological Bibliography of the Eastern Seaboard,* Eastern States Archeological Federation, *Research Pubn.* 1 (New Haven, 1947). 174 p., map.

Contains archeology, ethnology, and local history, classified and arranged geographically. Ethnic entities correlated to states, tribal classification, and synonymy. A compilation of references, often from other bibliographies and not from the books, but very useful.

Spiller, Robert E., Willard Thorp, Thomas H. Johnson, and Henry Seidel Canby, *Literary History of the United States,* Vol. III: *Bibliography* (N. Y., 1948). 817 p.

In addition to special sections on Indian captivities, Indian lore and antiquities, and Indian treaties, the *Lit. Hist.* bibliography gives bibliographies of 207 individual authors, many of whom dealt with Indian subjects.

Swanton, John R., *The Indian Tribes of North America,* Bur. Amer. Ethnol., *Bull.* 145 (Wash., 1952). 726 p., maps, bibliog.

A general summary of Swanton's knowledge of the continent and exposition of the method of ethnic entities, the work must be used with caution on some groups for which the sources are poor. Lacks documentation, but the extensive bibliography contains Swanton's principal monographs on Southeastern tribes, and those for the rest of the continent to about 1940. Locations are for the year 1650.

Swem, Earl G., *Virginia Historical Index* (Roanoke, 1934-1936). 2 vols.

This important work is an index to information that relates to Virginia and Virginians (including Indians) in the *Virginia Magazine of History and Biography,* Vols. 1-38 (1893-1930); the *William and Mary College Quarterly Historical Magazine,* 1st ser., Vols. 1-27 (1892-1919); the *William and Mary College Quarterly Historical Magazine,* 2nd ser., Vols. 1-10 (1921-1930); *Tyler's Quarterly Historical and Genealogical Magazine,* Vols. 1-10 (1919-1929); the *Virginia Historical Register and Literary Advertiser,* Vols. 1-6 (1848-1853); the *Lower Norfolk County Virginia Antiquary,* Vols. 1-5 (1895-1906); William W. Hening's *Statutes at Large, Being a Collection of All the Laws of Virginia, 1619-1792,* Vols. 1-13; and the *Calendar of State Papers and Other Manuscripts Preserved in the Capitol at Richmond, 1652-1869,* Vols. 1-11.

Trumbull, J. Hammond, "Books and Tracts in the Indian Language or Designed for the Use of the Indians, Printed at Cambridge and Boston, 1653-1721," Amer. Antiq. Soc., *Proceedings,* Oct. 21, 1873 (Worcester, 1874), pp. 45-62, with introductory comments, pp. 14-43.

Vail, Robert William G., *The Voice of the Old Frontier* (Phila., 1949). 492 p.

Contains 3 lectures given on the Rosenbach Fellowship in Bibliography at the Univ. of Penn.; "The Pioneer's Own Story," "The Indians' Captives Relate Their Adventures," and "The Frontier Land Agents Offer Their Wares", together with "A Bibliography of North American Frontier Literature [to 1800]," pp. 90-466, arranged chronologically by date of publication.

Winsor, Justin, ed., *Narrative and Critical History of America* (Boston and N. Y., 1884-1889). 8 vols., maps and other illus., bibliogs.

Vol. I (Aboriginal America); see esp. ch. 5 (George E. Ellis, "The Red Indian of North America in Contact with the French and English," with "Critical Essay" by Ellis and Winsor); ch. 6 (Henry W. Haynes, "The Prehistoric Archaeology of North America," and Justin Winsor, "The Progress of Opinion Respecting the Origin and Antiquity of Man in America"); appendix (a comprehensive bibliog. of aboriginal America by Winsor, pp. 413-444).

Vol. II (Spanish Explorations and Settlements); see esp. ch. 5 (George E. Ellis, "Las Casas, and the Relations of the Spaniards to the Indians," with "Critical Essay"); there are also chapters on Florida, Mexico, the Pacific Coast, and Peru and Chile.

Vol. IV (French Explorations and Settlements); see esp. ch. 6 (John Gilmary Shea, "The Jesuits, Recollects, and the Indians"); ch. 7 (Winsor, "The Jesuit Relations").

Vol. V (The English and French in North America); see esp. pp. 420-482 (Winsor on "Authorities on the French and Indian Wars of New England and Acadia, 1688-1763"); ch. 8 (Winsor, "The Struggle for the Great Valleys of North America," with "Critical Essay").

Vol. VI (The United States of North America); see esp. ch. 8 (Andrew McF. Davis, "The Indians and the Border Warfare of the Revolution," with "Critical Essay").

Winsor, Justin, "The New England Indians, 1630-1700," Mass. Hist. Soc., *Procs.*, 2d ser., 10 (1895-1896), 327-359.

List and discussion of 17th-century printed sources for the history of New England Indians.

Wolff, Hans, "Bibliography of Bibliographies of North American Indian Languages Still Spoken," *Inter. Jour. of Amer. Linguistics,* 13 (1947), 268-273.

Writings on American History: A Bibliography of Books and Articles on United States and Canadian History Published during the year 1902, (1904-   ), ed. Grace Gardner Griffin and others. Published in various places, 1904-1917, but from 1918 issued by the Government Printing Office as supplementary volumes to the *Annual Reports* of the Amer. Hist. Assoc. No volumes issued for 1941-1947, but publication was resumed, by the National Historical Publications Commission, with the volume for 1948 (Wash., 1952).

PART II

ETHNOLOGICAL LITERATURE

Beals, Ralph L., and Harry Hoijer, *An Introduction to Anthropology* (N. Y., 1953). 658 p., maps, illus.

> An elementary textbook for first and second-year college students who are beginning work in anthropology.

Beauchamp, William M., *Civil, Religious and Mourning Councils and Ceremonies of Adoption of the New York Indians,* N. Y. State Mus., *Bull.* 113 (Albany, 1906), 341-451, illus.

> Also printed separately, Albany, 1907.

Bidney, David, "The Concept of Value in Modern Anthropology," in Alfred L. Kroeber, ed., *Anthropology Today: An Encyclopedic Inventory* (Chicago, 1953), 682-699.

Boas, Franz, ed., *General Anthropology* (Boston, 1938). 718 p., illus., bibliog.

Boas, Franz, *Handbook of American Indian Languages,* Bur. Amer. Ethnol., *Bull.* 40, pts. 1-2 (Wash., 1911-1922). 1069, 903 p.

Boas, Franz, *The Mind of Primitive Man* (N. Y., 1938). 285 p., bibliog.

Brandt, Richard B., *Hopi Ethics: A Theoretical Analysis* (Chicago, 1954). 398 p., bibliog.

> Despite the extreme dissimilarity between the Hopi Indians and the Indians of the Eastern United States, this detailed study of Hopi ethics throws light on a subject too often neglected by colonial historians: that of Indian values.

Brinton, Daniel G., *The American Race: A Linguistic Classification and Ethnographic Description of the Native Tribes of North and South America* (N. Y., 1891). 392 p.

Brinton, Daniel G., *Essays of an Americanist* (Phila., 1890). 489 p., illus.

Brinton, Daniel G., *The Myths of the New World: A Treatise on the Symbolism and Mythology of the Red Race of America* (N. Y., 1868). 307 p.

Dockstader, Frederick J., *The Kachina and the White Man: A Study of the Influence of White Culture on the Hopi Kachina Cult,* Cranbrook Institute of Science, *Bull.* 35 (Bloomfield Hills, Mich., 1954). 185 p., illus., bibliog.

An excellent example of ethnohistorical research.

Driver, Harold E., John M. Cooper, Paul Kirchhoff, Dorothy Rainier Libby, William C. Massey, and Leslie Spier, *Indian Tribes of North America,* Ind. Univ., *Pubns. in Anthropol. and Linguistics, Memoir 9:* Supplement to *International Jour. of Amer. Linguistics,* 19 (1953). 30 p., maps.

The most up-to-date map of Indian tribal boundaries. Designed primarily as a cartographic tool "to facilitate the production of geographical distribution of racial, linguistic, and cultural data."

Eggan, Fred, "The Ethnological Cultures and Their Archeological Backgrounds," in James B. Griffin, ed., *Archeology of Eastern United States* (Chicago, 1952), 35-45.

Fenton, W. N., "Collecting Materials for a Political History of the Six Nations," Amer. Philos. Soc., *Procs.,* 93 (1949), 233-238.

Fenton, W. N., "An Iroquois Condolence Council for Installing Cayuga Chiefs in 1945," Wash. Acad. Sci., *Jour.,* 36 (1946), 110-127.

Field work undertaken while translating the Hewitt and Goldenweiser MSS produced a situation for observation of the central ceremony in Iroquois political life.

Fenton, W. N., "Iroquois Studies at the Mid-Century," Amer. Philos. Soc., *Procs.,* 95 (1951), 296-310.

Fenton, W. N., "The Present Status of Anthropology in Northeastern North America," *Amer. Anthropol.,* 50 (1948), 494-515, bibliog.

Fenton, W. N., "Problems Arising from the Historic Northeastern Position of the Iroquois," *Essays in Hist. Anthropol. of North America, Published in Honor of John R. Swanton . . . ,* Smithsonian Misc. *Colls.,* 100 (Wash., 1940), 159-251.

An exposition of the method of ethnic entities.

Fenton, W. N., *The Roll Call of the Iroquois Chiefs: A Study of a Mnemonic Cane from the Six Nations Reserve,* Smithsonian Misc. *Colls.,* 111 (Wash., 1950), 1-74, illus.

Documenting a museum specimen entailed field observation of a living ceremony and analysis of political organization to which it was the key.

Fenton, W. N., ed., *Symposium on Local Diversity in Iroquois Culture,*

Bur. Amer. Ethnol., *Bull.* 149 (Wash., 1951). 187 p., illus., bibliogs.
　　L. H. Morgan and Sir Henry Maine's concepts of kin and territory are re-examined by contemporary Iroquoianists.

Fenton, W. N., "The Training of Historical Ethnologists in America," *Amer. Anthropol.,* 54 (1952), 328-339.

Flannery, Regina, *An Analysis of Coastal Algonquian Culture,* Catholic Univ. of America, *Anthropol. Ser.,* No. 7 (Wash., 1939), 1-219.
　　A critical catalog of culture traits from historical and ethnological sources with inferences as to provenience.

Gilbert, William H., Jr., *The Eastern Cherokees,* Bur. Amer. Ethnol., *Bull.* 133, *Anthropol. Papers,* No. 23 (Wash., 1943), 169-413, illus.

Gilbert, William H., Jr., "Surviving Indian Groups of the Eastern United States," Smithsonian *Ann. Report,* 1948 (Wash., 1949), 407-438, map, bibliog.
　　Catalogs groups like the Wesorts of Maryland, Croatans of Carolina, with census data.

Guthe, Carl E., "Twenty-Five Years of Archeology in the Eastern United States," in James B. Griffin, ed., *Archeology of Eastern United States* (Chicago, 1952), 1-12.

Hallowell, Alfred Irving, "The Self and Its Behavioral Environment," in his *Culture and Experience* (Phila., 1955). 434 p., map, diagr.
　　From a humanistic point of view, an extraordinarily valuable introduction to the problems of getting at differing conceptions of the self.

Harrington, Mark R., "A Preliminary Sketch of Lenápe Culture," *Amer. Anthropol.,* 15 (1913), 208-235.

Harrington, Mark R., *Religion and Ceremonies of the Lenápe,* Mus. of Amer. Indian, Heye Foundation, *Indian Notes and Monographs,* No. 19 (N. Y., 1921). 249 p.

Havighurst, Robert J., and Bernice L. Neugarten, *American Indian and White Children: A Sociopsychological Investigation* (Chicago, 1955). 335 p.
　　One of a series (see MacGregor in this section). The purpose of this study was to investigate the moral, emotional, and intellectual development of Indian and white children in eight different localities. The book is a useful guide to Indian assumptions and values for the historian beginning the study of Indian-white relations.

Herskovits, Melville J., *Man and His Works: The Science of Cultural Anthropology* (N. Y., 1948). 716 p.

Hewitt, J. N. B., *Iroquoian Cosmology,* Bur. Amer. Ethnol., 21st *Ann. Report,* 1899-1900 (Wash., 1903), 129-339, illus.

Hoebel, E. Adamson, *The Law of Primitive Man: A Study in Comparative Legal Dynamics* (Cambridge, Mass., 1954). 357 p., bibliog.

Modern studies such as this one are showing that "primitive" law cannot be dismissed with the word "custom," but is more elaborate in structure than was formerly believed.

Hoijer, Harry, ed., *Language in Culture: Conference on the Interrelations of Language and Other Aspects of Culture* (Chicago, 1954). 286 p., bibliogs.

The report of a conference in which a group of specialists in linguistics, anthropology, philosophy, and psychology examined theories of Edward Sapir and Benjamin L. Whorf on how linguistic patterns and linguistic behavior condition *what* the individual perceives in his world and *how* he thinks about it. A study of assumptions and values as revealed in linguistic behavior is a "must" for the historian dealing with cultural relations.

[Hoijer, Harry, and others], *Linguistic Structures of Native America,* Viking Fund *Pubns. in Anthropol.,* No. 6 (N. Y., 1946). 423 p.

The best available summary of North American Indian languages and their relationships by the modern generation of the students of the late Edward Sapir: Hoijer, Swadesh, Bloomfield, Voegelin, Whorf, Halpern, Trager, Newman, Haas, Li.

Holmes, G. K., "Aboriginal Agriculture—The American Indians," in Liberty H. Bailey, ed., *Cyclopedia of American Agriculture* (2d edn., N. Y., 1909-1910), IV, 24-39, illus., bibliog.

An early but significant article.

Jenness, Diamond, *The Indians of Canada* (3d edn., Ottawa, 1955), National Museum of Canada, *Bull.* 65, Anthropological Series, No. 15. 452 p., maps, illus., bibliog.

First edn. 1932.

Johnson, Frederick, ed., *Man in Northeastern North America,* Robert S. Peabody Foundation for Archaeology, *Papers,* 3 (Andover, Mass., 1946). 347 p., maps, illus., bibliogs.

Kidd, Kenneth E., "Trade Goods Research Techniques," *Amer. Antiq.*, 20 (1954), 1-8.

An important bibliographic source for the study of European artifacts found on Indian sites.

Kinietz, William Vernon, *The Indians of the Western Great Lakes, 1615-1760,* Univ. Mich., Mus. Anthropol., *Occasional Contributions,* No. 10 (Ann Arbor, 1940). 427 p., map, bibliog.

Huron, Miami, Ottawa, Potawatomi, Chippewa; Appendix contains Antoine Denis Raudot's "Memoir" concerning the different Indian nations of North America.

Kluckhohn, Clyde, and Dorothea Leighton, *The Navaho* (Cambridge, Mass., 1946). 258 p., map, illus., bibliog.

Kluckhohn's method can well be emulated by the student of Indian culture in Eastern North America.

Knowles, Nathaniel, "The Torture of Captives by the Indians of Eastern North America," Amer. Philos. Soc., *Procs.,* 82 (1940), 151-225, bibliog.

Kroeber, Alfred L. *Anthropology: Race, Language, Culture, Psychology, Prehistory* (N. Y., 1948). 856 p., maps, illus., bibliog.

An important basic text.

Kroeber, A. L., and others, *Anthropology Today: An Encyclopedic Inventory* (Chicago, 1953). 966 p.

A collection of fifty papers written for the purpose of "inventorying" our knowledge of anthropology. Discussed in June 1952 at the International Symposium on Anthropology of the Wenner-Gren Foundation held in New York. For an account of the discussions based on these papers, see Tax and others, *An Appraisal of Anthropology Today,* and Thomas, *Current Anthropology,* later in this section.

Kroeber, A. L., *Cultural and Natural Areas of Native North America,* Univ. Calif., *Pubns. in Amer. Archaeol. and Ethnol.,* 38 (Berkeley, 1939). 242 p.

The best summary of ecological and historical relationships for the entire continent.

Kroeber, A. L., *Handbook of the Indians of California,* Bur. Amer. Ethnol., *Bull.* 78 (Wash., 1925). 995 p.

This is a classic and model treatment of an American culture area.

Kroeber, A. L., "The Work of John R. Swanton," *Essays in Hist. Anthropol. of North America,* Smithsonian *Misc. Colls.,* 100 (Wash., 1940), 1-10.

Le Clercq, Chrestien, *New Relation of Gaspesia, with the Customs and Religion of the Gaspesian Indians* [1691], trans. and ed. William F. Ganong (Toronto: The Champlain Society, 1910). 321 p. French text: 323-443.

Lilly, Eli, *Prehistoric Antiquities of Indiana* (Indianapolis, 1937). 293 p., illus., bibliog.

Linton, Ralph, *The Study of Man* (N. Y., 1936). 503 p.

Llewellyn, Karl N., and E. Adamson Hoebel, *The Cheyenne Way: Conflict and Case Law in Primitive Jurisprudence* (Norman, Okla., 1941). 360 p., illus.

    Second printing 1953. A classic study of the legal culture of an Indian tribe. Although it deals with Indians of the Great Plains it can help the historian in his study of the law-ways of Eastern tribes in the colonial period. It is, moreover, pertinent to a study of white legal institutions.

Lowie, Robert H., *The History of Ethnological Theory* (N. Y., 1937). 296 p.

MacGregor, Gordon, *Warriors without Weapons: A Study of the Society and Personality Development of the Pine Ridge Sioux* (Chicago, 1946). 228 p., map, illus., bibliog.

    This volume is one of several studies of Indian personality undertaken jointly by the Committee on Human Development of the University of Chicago and the United States Office of Indian Affairs.

Macleod, William Christie, "The Family Hunting Territory and Lenápe Political Organization," *Amer. Anthropol.,* 24 (1922), 448-463.

Mahr, August C., "Eighteenth Century Terminology of Delaware Indian Cultivation and Use of Maize: A Semantic Analysis," *Ethnohistory,* 2 (1955), 209-240.

Malinowski, Bronislaw, *Argonauts of the Western Pacific* (London, 1922). 527 p., maps, illus.

    An anthropological "classic."

Martin, Paul S., George I. Quimby, and Donald Collier, *Indians before Columbus: Twenty Thousand Years of North American History*

Revealed by Archeology (Chicago, 1947). 582 p., map, illus., glossary, bibliog.

A good survey "for the interested layman and for students taking introductory courses in anthropology." Since most historians lack anthropological training, they can profitably begin their study of Indian archeology with such a book.

Mead, Margaret, *The Changing Culture of an Indian Tribe* (N. Y., 1932). 313 p.

Margaret Mead's study of modern culture contact helps the historian understand the process of colonial culture contact for which evidence, in the modern sense, no longer exists.

Mook, Maurice A., "The Aboriginal Population of Tidewater Virginia," *Amer. Anthropol.,* 46 (1944), 193-208.

Mook, Maurice A., "Algonkian Ethnohistory of the Carolina Sound," Wash. Acad. Sci., *Jour.,* 34 (1944), 181-197; 213-228.

Mook, Maurice A., "The Anthropological Position of the Indian Tribes of Tidewater Virginia," *William and Mary College Quart.,* 2d ser., 23 (1943), 27-40.

Mook, Maurice A., "The Ethnological Significance of Tindall's Map of Virginia, 1608," *William and Mary College Quart.,* 2d ser., 23 (1943), 371-408.

Mook, Maurice A., "Virginia Ethnology from an Early Relation," *William and Mary College Quart.,* 2d ser., 23 (1943), 101-129.

Mooney, James, *The Ghost-dance Religion and the Sioux Outbreak of 1890,* Bur. Amer. Ethnol., 14th *Ann. Report,* 1892-1893, pt. 2 (Wash., 1896), 641-1136, maps, illus., bibliog.

An important landmark in historical ethnology, commencing in the Eastern Woodlands and extending to the Plains.

Mooney, James, *Myths of the Cherokee,* Bur. Amer. Ethnol., 19th *Ann. Report,* 1897-1898, pt. 1 (Wash., 1900), 3-568, maps, illus.

Mooney's long historical sketch of the Cherokee, and the notes on the sketch, have reference value to historians of intertribal relations, locations, and movements in the Appalachians.

Mooney, James, *The Sacred Formulas of the Cherokees,* Bur. Amer. Ethnol., 7th *Ann. Report,* 1885-1886 (Wash., 1891), 301-397, illus.

Mooney, James, *The Siouan Tribes of the East,* Bur. Amer. Ethnol., *Bull.* 22 (Wash., 1894). 101 p., map.

The first exposition of the method of ethnic entities. But for Mooney, our knowledge of the extinct eastern Siouans would be nihil.

Mooney, James, and Frans M. Olbrechts, eds., *The Swimmer Manuscript: Cherokee Sacred Formulas and Medicinal Prescriptions,* Bur. Amer. Ethnol., *Bull.* 99 (Wash., 1932). 319 p., illus., bibliog.

Morgan, Lewis H., *League of the Ho-dé-no-sau-nee, or Iroquois* (Rochester, 1851). 477 p., map, illus.

> Second edn., N. Y., 1901.

> The classic account of the Iroquois and considered the first ethnography of any living primitive people; concentrates on the Seneca where Morgan did his main field work after 1847; but weak on history and the beginnings of the League. H. M. Lloyd's notes to the 2nd edn. are highly useful.

Murdock, George Peter, and others, *Outline of Cultural Materials,* Yale Univ., Institute Human Relations, *Cross Cultural Survey* (New Haven, 1938). 55 p., index.

> 3rd revised edition: *Behavioral Science Outlines,* 1, Human Relations Area Files, Inc. (New Haven, 1950). 162 p.

> For simpler cultures the first edition is more adaptable. But later editions are better for special topics.

Murdock, George Peter, "The Processing of Anthropological Materials," in Kroeber and others, *Anthropology Today: An Encyclopedic Inventory* (Chicago, 1953), 476-487.

Nelson, Nels Christian, "The Antiquity of Man in America in the Light of Archeology," Smithsonian *Ann. Report,* 1935 (Wash., 1936), 471-506.

"Newberry Library Conference on Indian Studies," Newberry Libr., *Bull.,* 3 (1952), 30-36.

Newcomb, William W., Jr., *The Culture and Acculturation of the Delaware Indians,* Univ. Mich., Mus. Anthropol., *Anthropol. Papers,* No. 10 (Ann Arbor, 1956). 141 p., map, illus., bibliog.

Noon, John A., *Law and Government of the Grand River Iroquois,* Viking Fund *Pubns. in Anthropol.,* No. 12 (N. Y., 1949). 186 p.

> The proceedings and decisions of the Council as recorded in minutes until 1924 were searched for trouble cases still remembered

by veterans of the Old Council who strive to reconcile old values with changing circumstances of Indian life today.

Parker, Arthur C., *The Code of Handsome Lake, the Seneca Prophet,* N. Y. State Mus., *Bull.* 163 (Albany, 1913). 148 p.

The most sought-after ethnological report of the Longhouse Iroquois today, now out-of-print; but A. F. C. Wallace's forthcoming biography of Handsome Lake will find a ready reception among students of Indian culture.

Parker, Arthur C., *The Archeological History of New York,* N. Y. State Mus., *Bull.* 235-238 (Albany, 1922). 2 vols., maps, illus.

Parker, Arthur C., *The Constitution of the Five Nations or the Iroquois Book of the Great Law,* N. Y. State Mus., *Bull.* 184 (Albany, 1916). 158 p., map, illus.

Also printed separately, Albany, 1916.

Parker, Arthur C., "The Influence of the Iroquois on the History and Archaeology of the Wyoming Valley and the Adjacent Region," Wyoming [Co., Pa.] Historical and Geological Society, Wilkes-Barre, Pa., *Procs. and Colls.,* 11 (1910), 65-102, illus.

Also printed separately, Wilkes-Barre, 1911.

Powell, John W., *Indian Linguistic Families of America, North of Mexico,* Bur. Amer. Ethnol., 7th *Ann. Report,* 1885-1886 (Wash., 1891), 1-142, map.

Radcliffe-Brown, Alfred Reginald, *Structure and Function in Primitive Society: Essays and Addresses.* Foreword by E. E. Evans-Pritchard and Fred Eggan (London, 1952). 219 p., illus.

Radin, Paul, *The Winnebago Tribe,* Bur. Amer. Ethnol., 37th *Ann. Report,* 1915-1916 (Wash., 1923), 35-560.

Rainey, Froelich G., "A Compilation of Historical Data Contributing to the Ethnography of Connecticut and Southern New England Indians," Archaeol. Soc. Conn., *Bull.* 3 (New Haven, 1936), 1-90, bibliog.

Redfield, Robert, *The Primitive World and Its Transformations* (Ithaca, N. Y., 1953). 185 p.

The Messenger Lectures on the Evolution of Civilization, Cornell University, 1952. Redfield discusses the "moral order" in early societies and the causes of changing ethical judgments.

Sapir, Edward, "Time Perspective in Aboriginal American Culture: A

Study in Method," Canada *Geol. Survey,* Anthropol. Ser., 13 (Ottawa, 1916), 1-87.

Reprinted in D. G. Mandelbaum, ed., *Selected Writings of Edward Sapir* (Berkeley and Los Angeles, 1949), 389-462.

Shetrone, Henry Clyde, *The Mound-Builders* . . . (N. Y., 1930). 508 p., maps, illus., bibliog.

Snyderman, George S., *Behind the Tree of Peace: A Sociological Analysis of Iroquois Warfare* (Phila., 1948). 93 p., bibliog.

Snyderman, George S., "Concepts of Land Ownership among the Iroquois and Their Neighbors," in Fenton, ed., *Symposium on Local Diversity in Iroquois Culture,* Bur. Amer. Ethnol., *Bull.* 149 (1951), 13-34.

Snyderman, George S., "The Functions of Wampum," Amer. Philos. Soc., *Procs.,* 98 (1954), 469-494.

Sorokin, Pitirim A., *Social and Cultural Dynamics,* especially Vol. II: *Fluctuations of Systems of Truth, Ethics, and Law,* and Vol. III: *Fluctuation of Social Relationships, War, and Revolution* (N. Y., 1937). 727, 636 p.

Anyone dealing intelligently with Indian-white relations cannot write from his own particular assumptions concerning truth, ethics, law, and social relationships in general. Sorokin's analysis of "ideational," "idealistic," and "sensate" cultures cannot be overlooked by the student of culture contact.

Speck, Frank G., "Bird Nomenclature and Song Interpretation of the Canadian Delaware: An Essay in Ethnoornithology," Wash. Acad. Sci., *Jour.,* 36 (1946), 249-258.

Speck, Frank G., *The Celestial Bear Comes Down to Earth: The Bear Sacrifice Ceremony of the Munsee-Mahican in Canada as Related by Neḳatcit,* Reading Public Mus. and Art Gallery, *Sci. Pubns.,* No. 7 (Reading, Penna., 1945). 91 p., illus.

Speck, Frank G., *Chapters on the Ethnology of the Powhatan Tribes of Virginia,* Mus. Amer. Indian, Heye Foundation, *Indian Notes and Monographs,* 1 (1928), 225-455, maps, illus.

Authoritative essay on feather-work fabrics in Eastern North America, recovered from living members of the tribes as well as from documentary sources, illustrating how cultural memory sheds light on history.

Speck, Frank G., "Culture Problems in Northeastern North America," Amer. Philos. Soc., *Procs.,* 65 (1926), 272-311.

Speck's name is almost synonymous with the ethnology of the Algonquian peoples of Eastern North America and of their Iroquoian neighbors, particularly the Cayuga, and the Cherokee in the highlands of Carolina. See also Speck's "The Ethnic Position of the Southeastern Algonkian," *Amer. Anthropol.,* 26 (1924), 184-200; and his obituary by A. I. Hallowell, *Amer. Anthropol.,* 53 (1951), 67-75, with bibliog. by John Witthoft, 75-87.

Speck, Frank G., "Ethnoherpetology of the Catawba and Cherokee Indians," Wash. Acad. Sci., *Jour.,* 36 (1946), 355-360.

Speck, Frank G., "The Nanticoke Community of Delaware," Mus. Amer. Indian, Heye Foundation, *Contributions,* 2, No. 4 (N. Y., 1915). 43 p.

Speck, Frank G., *Native Tribes and Dialects of Connecticut: A Mohegan-Pequot Diary,* Bur. Amer. Ethnol., 43rd *Ann. Report,* 1925-1926 (Wash., 1928), 199-287, maps, illus.

Speck, Frank G., *Oklahoma Delaware Ceremonies, Feasts and Dances,* Amer. Philos. Soc., *Memoirs,* 7 (Phila., 1937), 1-161.

Speck, Frank G., *Penobscot Man* (Phila., 1940). 325 p., illus.

Speck, Frank G., "The Rappahannock Indians of Virginia," Mus. Amer. Indian, Heye Foundation, *Indian Notes and Monographs,* 5 (N. Y., 1925), 25-83, illus.

Speck, Frank G., "Siouan Tribes of the Carolinas as Known from Catawba, Tutelo, and Documentary Sources," *Amer. Anthropol.,* 37 (1935), 201-225.

Speck, Frank G., *A Study of the Delaware Indian Big House Ceremony,* Penna. Hist. Comm., *Pubns.,* 2 (Harrisburg, 1931). 192 p.

Speck, Frank G., *Territorial Subdivisions and Boundaries of the Wampanoag, Massachusetts, and Nauset Indians,* Mus. Amer. Indian, Heye Foundation, *Indian Notes and Monographs,* 44 (N. Y., 1928), 7-152.

Stern, Theodore, "Chickahominy: The Changing Culture of a Virginia Indian Community," Amer. Philos. Soc., *Procs.,* 96 (1952), 157-225, bibliog.

Stern uses both historical and ethnological sources, period by period, to outline and describe cultural climax and decline since colonial times.

Strong, William Duncan, "Historical Approach in Anthropology," in Alfred L. Kroeber, ed., *Anthropology Today: An Encyclopedic Inventory* (Chicago, 1953), 386-397, bibliog.

Strong was an early exponent of the method of using the ethnological present to throw light on the archeological past.

Swadesh, Morris, "Lexico-Statistic Dating of Prehistoric Ethnic Contacts: With Special Reference to North American Indians and Eskimos," Amer. Philos. Soc., *Procs.,* 96 (1952), 452-463.

Swanton, John R., *Early History of the Creek Indians and Their Neighbors,* Bur. Amer. Ethnol., *Bull.* 73 (Wash., 1922). 492 p., maps.

Using both documentary and living sources on the Creek Confederacy, Swanton presents a historical introduction to ethnological studies published in 42d *Ann. Report* of the Bureau.

[Swanton, John R., Chairman], *Final Report of the United States De Soto Expedition Commission,* H.R. Document No. 71, 76th Congress, 1st Session (Wash., 1939). 400 p., maps., bibliog.

Swanton, John R., *Indian Tribes of the Lower Mississippi Valley and Adjacent Coast of the Gulf of Mexico,* Bur. Amer. Ethnol., *Bull.* 43 (Wash., 1911). 387 p., map, illus.

Swanton's pioneer and basic work in ethnohistory; ethnography of the Natchez from documentary sources.

Swanton, John R., *The Indians of the Southeastern United States,* Bur. Amer. Ethnol., *Bull.* 137 (Wash., 1946). 943 p., maps, illus., bibliog.

Geography, population, history, and ethnology of the ethnic entities of the Southeast. Includes extensive quotations from sources on material culture, with some account of social and ceremonial usages not previously reported in Swanton's monographs. The handbook on the Southeast.

Swanton, John R., "Notes on the Mental Assimilation of Races," Wash. Acad. Sci., *Jour.,* 16 (Wash., 1926), 493-502.

Tax, Sol, Loren C. Eiseley, Irving Rouse, and Carl F. Voegelin, eds., *An Appraisal of Anthropology Today* (Chicago, 1953). 395 p.

An edited transcript of the discussions that took place at the International Symposium on Anthropology of the Wenner-Gren Foundation held in New York in June 1952. For the papers which provided the basis for the discussion, see Kroeber, *Anthropology Today,* earlier in this section.

Thomas, William L., Jr., ed., *Current Anthropology: A Supplement to Anthropology Today* (Chicago, 1956). 377 p.

Nineteen scholars contribute essays which supplement those in Kroeber, *Anthropology Today.*

Trager, George L., "An Outline of Taos Grammar," in Harry Hoijer, ed., *Linguistic Structures of Native America* (N. Y., 1946), pp. 184-221.

Trowbridge, Charles C., *Shawnese Traditions,* ed. Vernon Kinietz and Erminie W. Voegelin, Univ. Mich., Mus. Anthropol., *Occasional Contributions,* No. 9 (Ann Arbor, 1939). 71 p.

Valinger, Leon de, Jr., and C. A. Weslager, "Indian Land Sales in Delaware." With addendum, "A Discussion of the Family Hunting Territory Question in Delaware," by C. A. Weslager, Arch. Soc. Del., *Bull.* (Wilmington, 1941), 1-13, 14-24.

Voegelin, Charles F., "North American Indian Languages Still Spoken and Their Genetic Relationships," in Leslie Spier, A. Irving Hallowell, and Stanley S. Neuman, eds., *Language, Culture, and Personality: Essays in Honor of Edward Sapir* (Menasha, Wis., 1941), pp. 15-40.

Voegelin, Erminie Wheeler, "Mortuary Customs of the Shawnee and Other Eastern Tribes," Ind. Hist. Soc., *Prehistory Research Ser.,* 2 (Indianapolis, 1944), 227-444, bibliog.

A model of ethnological and historical analysis of cultural materials for purposes of comparing complexes and drawing inferences of relationships in time and space. Critical notes on sources. Bibliography of manuscripts and printed sources, pp. 423-429, 433-444.

Wallace, Anthony F. C., *The Modal Personality Structure of the Tuscarora Indians, as Revealed by the Rorschach Tests,* Bur. Amer. Ethnol., *Bull.* 150 (Wash., 1952). 120 p., illus., bibliog.

Wallis, Wilson D., and Ruth Sawtell Wallis, *The Micmac Indians of Eastern Canada* (Minneapolis, 1955). 515 p., illus., bibliogs.

Waugh, Frederick Wilkenson, *Iroquois Food and Food Preparation* (Ottawa, 1916). 235 p., illus., bibliog.

Wedel, Waldo Rudolph, "The Direct-historical Approach in Pawnee

Archeology," Smithsonian *Misc. Colls.*, 97, No. 7 (Wash., 1938). 21 p., illus.

Wedel, Waldo Rudolph, *An Introduction to Pawnee Archeology,* Bur. Amer. Ethnol., *Bull.* 112 (Wash., 1936). 122 p., illus., bibliog.

Weslager, Clinton A., *Delaware's Buried Past: A Story of Archaelogical Adventure* (Phila., 1944). 170 p., map, bibliog.

    Valuable bibliography of local archaeology and surviving Indians: Nanticoke, Delaware, etc.

Weslager, Clinton A., *Delaware's Forgotten Folk: The Story of the Moors and Nanticokes* (Phila., 1943). 215 p., map, illus., bibliog.

Whorf, Benjamin L., *Language, Thought, and Reality: Selected Writings,* ed. John B. Carroll (Cambridge, 1956). 278 p., illus., bibliog.

Willoughby, Charles C., *Antiquities of the New England Indians, with Notes on the Ancient Cultures of the Adjacent Territory* (Cambridge, Mass.: Peabody Mus. of Amer. Archeol. and Ethnol., Harvard Univ., 1935). 314 p., illus.

Wissler, Clark, *The American Indian: An Introduction to the Anthropology of the New World* (3d edn., N. Y., 1938). 466 p., maps, illus., bibliog.

    First edn. N. Y., 1917. Still the best general classification and description of the content of ethnological areas; weak on archeology.

Wissler, Clark, "The American Indian and the American Philosophical Society," Amer. Philos. Soc., *Procs.*, 86 (1942), 189-204.

    A schema for the history of American anthropology.

Wissler, Clark, *Ceremonial Bundles of the Blackfoot Indians,* Amer. Mus. Natural Hist., *Anthropol. Papers,* 7, pt. 2 (N. Y., 1912), 1-298.

Wissler, Clark, *Indians of the United States: Four Centuries of Their History and Culture,* Amer. Mus. Natural Hist., *Sci. Ser.* (N. Y., 1940). 319 p.

    Wissler abandoned the culture area approach for the advancing frontier as a frame of reference, treating groups by language families. A popular and highly suggestive book, but lacking in the rigor of his earlier work.

Wissler, Clark, "Material Culture of the Blackfoot Indians," Amer. Mus. Natural Hist., *Anthropol. Papers,* 5, pt. 1 (N. Y., 1910), 1-175, bibliog.

Wissler made important use of documentary history for direct dating and for comparative purposes, setting a standard that was followed in American ethnology by Lowie, Spier, Skinner, and others who were associated with him on the Plains.

Wissler, Clark, "The Social Life of the Blackfoot Indians," Amer. Mus. Natural Hist., *Anthropol. Papers,* 7, pt. 1 (N. Y., 1911), 1-64, bibliog.

Witthoft, John, "The American Indian as Hunter," *Pennsylvania Game News,* 24 (1953), No. 2, 12-16; No. 3, 17-22; No. 4, 8-13; illus.
    Also issued as Reprints in Anthropology from the Pennsylvania Historical and Museum Commission, [Harrisburg], No. 6.

Witthoft, John, "An Early Cherokee Ethnobotanical Note," Wash. Acad. Sci., *Jour.,* 37 (1947), 73-75.

Witthoft, John, "Bird Lore of the Eastern Cherokee," Wash. Acad. Sci., *Jour.,* 36 (1946), 372-384.

Witthoft, John, "Some Eastern Cherokee Bird Stories," Wash. Acad. Sci., *Jour.,* 36 (1946), 177-180.

Witthoft, John, "Green Corn Ceremonialism in the Eastern Woodlands," Univ. Mich., Mus. Anthropol., *Occasional Contributions,* No. 13 (Ann Arbor, 1949), 1-91.

PART III

HISTORICAL LITERATURE

A. Before 1850

Adair, James, *The History of the American Indians, Particularly Those Nations Adjoining to the Mississippi, East and West Florida, Georgia, South and North Carolina, and Virginia* . . . (London, 1775). 464 p., map.

Repr. Johnson City, Tenn., 1930, ed. Samuel C. Williams. "Standard work on the Southern Indians by a famous Indian trader and frontiersman who was one of the first to explore the Alleghanies" (Vail 643).

Barton, Benjamin Smith, *New Views of the Origin of the Tribes and Nations of America* (Phila., 1797). 83 p.

A pioneer work on Indian linguistics.

Bartram, John, *Observations on the Inhabitants, Climate, Soil, Rivers, Productions, Animals, and Other Matters Worthy of Notice,* . . . *in His Travels from Pensilvania to Onondago, Oswego, and the Lake Ontario, in Canada* . . . (London, 1751). 94 p., illus.

Repr. Geneva, N. Y., 1895.

Bartram, William, "Travels in Georgia and Florida, 1773-74. A Report to Dr. John Fothergill," ed. Francis Harper, Amer. Philos. Soc., *Trans.,* 33 (1942-1943), 121-242, maps, illus., facsims., bibliog.

Here printed from the MS in the British Museum and thus more reliable and far fresher than Bartram's famous *Travels.*

Bartram, William, *Travels through North and South Carolina, Georgia, East & West Florida, the Cherokee Country, the Extensive Territories of the Muscogulges, or Creek Confederacy, and the Country of the Chactaws* . . . (Phila., 1791). 522 p., map., illus.

Frequently reprinted and translated; Mark Van Doren edited *The Travels of William Bartram* (N. Y., 1928 and 1940).

Beverley, Robert, *The History and Present State of Virginia,* ed. Louis B. Wright (Chapel Hill, N. C., 1947). 366 p., illus.

Originally pubd. London, 1705, revised edn. 1722. Book III is a classic description of "The Native Indians, Their Religion, Laws, and Customs, in War and Peace."

Boucher, Pierre, *Histoire véritable et naturelle des moeurs et productions du pays de la Nouvelle France, vulgairement dite le Canada* (Paris, 1664). 168 p.

A later edn., Montreal, 1882.

Bradford, William, *Of Plymouth Plantation, 1620-1647,* ed. Samuel Eliot Morison (N. Y., 1952). 448 p., maps.

A modern edition of Governor Bradford's classic story of the founding of the colony, first published from the MS, Boston, 1856; there are several other editions.

Byrd, William, *Histories of the Dividing Line Betwixt Virginia and North Carolina* [as run in 1728-1729], ed. William K. Boyd (Raleigh, 1929). 341 p., maps.

Byrd's *History* and other writings were edited by Thomas H. Wynne, 2 vols. (Richmond, 1866), and by John Spencer Bassett (N. Y., 1901).

Campbell, William W., *Annals of Tryon County; or, The Border Warfare of New-York, during the Revolution* (N. Y., 1831). 191, 78 p., map.

An enlarged edn. was issued under the title of *The Border Warfare of New-York . . .* (N. Y., 1849). 396 p.

Carver, Jonathan, *Travels through the Interior Parts of North America, in the Years 1766, 1767, and 1768* (London, 1778). 543 p., maps, illus.

Numerous later edns. Like other narrators of adventures among the Indians, Carver is not entirely trustworthy.

Champlain, Samuel de, *The Works of,* trans. and ed. H. P. Biggar and others (Toronto, 1922-1936). 6 vols., maps, illus., facsims.

Charlevoix, Pierre F. X. de, *History and General Description of New France,* trans. John Gilmary Shea (N. Y., 1866-1872). 6 vols., maps, illus., facsims.

First pubd. Paris, 1744. Another edn. of Shea's Charlevoix, N. Y., 1900.

Church, Benjamin, *The History of King Philip's War . . .,* ed. Samuel G. Drake (Boston, 1825). 304 p.

First pubd. Boston, 1716, with title *Entertaining Passages Relating to Philip's War . . .;* numerous other edns.

Clark, Joshua V. H., *Onondaga; or, Reminiscences of Earlier and Later Times; Being a Series of Historical Sketches Relative to Onondaga; with Notes on the Several Towns in the County, and Oswego* (Syracuse, 1849). 2 vols., map, illus.

> Vol. I is largely devoted to the Indian history of central New York; "in fact a history of the Onondaga tribe of the Six Nations" (Field 323).

Clinton, DeWitt, *Discourse Delivered before the New-York Historical Society, . . . 6th December, 1811* (N. Y., 1812). 81 p.

> Also in N. Y. Hist. Soc., *Colls.,* 2 (1811-1859), 37-116. "A general geographical, political and historical view of the red men who inhabited this state" (p.6).

Colden, Cadwallader, *The History of the Five Indian Nations Depending on the Province of New-York,* ed. John Gilmary Shea (N. Y., 1866). 141 p. (octavo).

> Originally pubd. N. Y., 1727, and reprinted London, 1747, and 1750. The 1866 edn. contains a valuable historical introduction and notes.

Craig, Neville B., ed., *The Olden Time* . . . (Cincinnati, 1876). 2 vols.

> Originally published as a periodical, Pittsburgh, 1846-1848. Valuable for documents relative to military and Indian affairs in the upper Ohio valley.

Doddridge, Joseph, *Notes on the Settlement and Indian Wars of the Western Parts of Virginia & Pennsylvania, from the Year 1763 until the Year 1783* . . . (Wellsburgh, Va., 1824). 316 p.

Drake, Samuel G., ed., *The Old Indian Chronicle; Being a Collection of Exceeding Rare Tracts, Written and Published in the Time of King Philip's War* (Boston, 1867). 333 p., map.

> An enlarged edn. of Drake's *The Old Indian Chronicle* (Boston, 1836); present edn. contains reprints of 7 tracts first printed in London, 1675-1676, with an extensive introduction by Drake on King Philip's War. Four of the tracts are included in C. H. Lincoln's edn. of *Narratives of the Indian Wars (Original Narratives of Early Amer. Hist.).* For other Drake entries see under Biography (§ VII, C).

Elvas, Gentleman of, *True Relation of the Hardships Suffered by Governor Fernando de Soto . . . during the Discovery of the Providence of Florida . . .*, trans. and ed. James A. Robertson (DeLand, Fla., 1933). 2 vols.

> First edn. 1557. An earlier English translation will be found in Frederick W. Hodge and Theodore L. Hodge, eds., *Spanish Explorers in the Southern United States* (N. Y., 1907), pp. 127-272. See also John R. Swanton, "Ethnological Value of the DeSoto Narratives," *Amer. Anthropol.*, 34 (1932), 570-590.

Filson, John, *The Discovery, Settlement and Present State of Kentucke . . .*, ed. Willard R. Jillson (Louisville, 1929). 198 p., maps., bibliog.

> A facsimile reproduction of original edn. pubd. Wilmington, Del., 1784. "The most famous and important frontier book of the period, by a frontiersman who was later killed by the Indians. Particularly important for its first map of Kentucky and its first published life of Daniel Boone" (Vail 694).

Flint, Timothy, *Indian Wars of the West* (Cincinnati, 1833). 240 p.

Foster, Sir Augustus John, *Jeffersonian America: Notes on the United States of America Collected in the Years 1805-6-7 and 11-12*, ed. Richard Beale Davis (San Marino, Calif., 1954). 356 p.

> This British diplomat was deeply interested in "the wild natives of the woods" wherever he observed them, and had much to say in his lively journal about Indian character and manners, government Indian policy, etc.

Gallatin, Albert, *A Synopsis of the Indian Tribes within the United States East of the Rocky Mountains, and in the British and Russian Possessions in North America*, Amer. Antiq. Soc., *Archaeologia Americana (Trans. and Colls.)*, 2 (1836), 7-422.

Garcilaso de la Vega, *The Florida of the Inca*, trans. and ed. John G. and Jeannette J. Varner (Austin, Tex., 1951). 655 p., map.

Gookin, Daniel, *An Historical Account of the Doings and Sufferings of the Christian Indians in New England, in the Years 1675, 1676, 1677 . . .*, Amer. Antiq. Soc., *Archaeologia Americana (Trans. and Colls.)*, 2 (1836), 423-534.

> Written 1677. Gookin was the protector of the Christian Indians during King Philip's War.

Gookin, Daniel, *Historical Collections of the Indians in New England. Of Their Several Nations, Numbers, Customs, Manners, Religion, and Government, before the English Planted There ...,* Mass. Hist. Soc., *Colls.,* 1st ser., 1 (1792), 141-232.

> Repr. separately, Boston, 1792. Originally written 1674.

Halkett, John, *Historical Notes Respecting the Indians of North America: with Remarks on the Attempts Made to Convert and Civilize Them* (London, 1825). 408 p.

> An early attempt to narrate the history of Indian relations with Europeans in North America.

Harrison, William Henry, *A Discourse on the Aborigines of the Ohio Valley ...* (Chicago, 1883). 95 p.

> First published in Hist. and Philos. Soc. of Ohio, *Trans.,* 1, pt. 2 (1839), 217-267.

Haywood, John, *The Civil and Political History of the State of Tennessee, from Its Earliest Settlement up to the Year 1796 ...* (Knoxville, Tenn., 1823). 504 p.

Haywood, John, *The Natural and Aboriginal History of Tennessee, up to the First Settlements Therein by the White People* (Nashville, Tenn., 1823). 390, 51 p.

Heckewelder, John G. E., *An Account of the History, Manners and Customs of the Indian Nations, Who Once Inhabited Pennsylvania and the Neighboring States* (Phila., 1819). 347 p.

> Rev. edn. ed. by Rev. William C. Reichel, in Hist. Soc. Penna., *Memoirs,* 12 (Phila., 1876), 47-465. An important source for Fenimore Cooper's Indian fiction.

Hennepin, Louis, *A New Discovery of a Vast Country in America ...,* ed. Reuben G. Thwaites (Chicago, 1903). 2 vols., illus., maps.

> Hennepin, a Recollect missionary, first published an account of his travels in the New World in Paris, 1683. The first English edn., differing in many ways from the original edn., was published in London, 1698.

Henry, Alexander, *Travels and Adventures in Canada and the Indian Territories between the Years 1760 and 1776* (N. Y., 1809). 330 p.

> Adventures of a fur-trader captured by the Indians.

Hildreth, Samuel P., *Pioneer History: Being an Account of the First Examinations of the Ohio Valley, and the Early Settlement of the Northwest Territory ...* (Cincinnati and N. Y., 1848). 525 p., maps, illus.

> Valuable for its documents.

Hough, Franklin B., ed., *Diary of the Siege of Detroit in the War with Pontiac. Also a Narrative of the Principal Events of the Siege, by Major Robert Rogers* . . . (Albany, 1860). 304 p.

Hoyt, Epaphras, *Antiquarian Researches: Comprising a History of the Indian Wars in the Country Bordering Connecticut River and Parts Adjacent* (Greenfield, Mass., 1824). 312 p.

Hubbard, William, *The History of the Indian Wars in New England, from the First Settlement to the Termination of the War with King Philip, in 1677,* ed. Samuel G. Drake (Roxbury, Mass., 1865). 2 vols.

> Originally published at Boston, 1677 (*A Narrative of the Troubles with the Indians in New-England*), and at London, also 1677 (*The Present State of New-England, Being a Narrative,* etc.); see Field 730, 731.

Hutchins, Thomas, *A Topographical Description of Virginia, Pennsylvania, Maryland, and North Carolina, Comprehending the Rivers Ohio, Kenhawa, Sioto, Cherokee, Wabash, Illinois, Mississippi, &c.* . . . (London, 1778). 67 p., plans, table.

> Hutchins prepared *A New Map of the Western Parts of Virginia, Pennsylvania, Maryland and North Carolina* . . . to accompany this work, but it was separately published.

Imlay, Gilbert, *A Topographical Description of the Western Territory of North America* . . . (3d edn., London, 1797). 598 p., maps.

> First pubd. 1792; 3d edn. is much expanded. Relates especially to the Kentucky country; contains reprints of Filson's *History of Kentucky,* Hutchins' *Topographical Descriptions,* etc.

Jefferson, Thomas, *Notes on the State of Virginia,* ed. William Peden (Chapel Hill, 1955). 315 p., map, illus.

> Privately printed, Paris, 1785; published London, 1787; numerous later editions, including reprints in Jefferson's collected works. Query XI treats "Aborigines" and is remarkably comprehensive. Query VI contains Jefferson's elaborate refutation of the thesis of Buffon and others that the human race degenerates in the New World. For Jefferson's Indian speeches as governor of Virginia and president of the U. S., see Andrew A. Lipscomb and Albert E. Bergh, eds., *The Writings of Thomas Jefferson* (Wash., 1903), XVI, 371-472. Jefferson's interest in and policy toward the Indians deserve a comprehensive study not yet written.

Jones, Hugh, *The Present State of Virginia, From Whence Is Inferred A Short View of Maryland and North Carolina* [1724], ed. Richard L. Morton (Chapel Hill, 1956). 295 p., illus.

Kenton, Edna, ed., *The Indians of North America, . . . Selected from "The Jesuit Relations and Allied Documents . . . 1610-1791"* (N. Y., 1925). 2 vols., maps, illus.

    New edn., N. Y., 1954., 1 vol. A selection of descriptive and narrative material from the great Thwaites edn. of *The Jesuit Relations.*

Lafitau, Joseph-François, *Moeurs des sauvages amériquains, comparées aux moeurs des premiers temps* (Paris, 1724). 2 vols. 610 p., 490 p.

    Repr. Paris, 1874. A critical edn. in English of this important work is being prepared by W. N. Fenton and Elizabeth L. Moore.

Lahontan, Louis A., Baron de, *New Voyages to North America,* ed. Reuben G. Thwaites (Chicago, 1905). 2 vols., maps, illus.

    First French and English edns., 1703.

Lawson, John, *The History of Carolina, Containing the Exact Description and Natural History of That Country, Together with the Present State Thereof and a Journal of a Thousand Miles Traveled through the Several Nations of Indians . . .* (Raleigh, N. C., 1860). 390 p.

    First published London, 1709, as *A New Voyage to Carolina . . .;* another reprint was published at Richmond, 1937.

Lescarbot, Marc, *The History of New France,* trans. W. L. Grant (Toronto, 1907-1914). 3 vols., maps.

    Champlain Soc. edn.; 1st edn., Paris, 1612.

Lindeström, Peter, *Geographia Americae, with an Account of the Delaware Indians, Based on Surveys and Notes Made in 1654-1656,* trans. and ed. Amandus Johnson (Phila., 1925). 418 p., illus., maps, facsims., bibliog.

Long, John, *Voyages and Travels in the Years 1768-1788,* ed. Milo M. Quaife (Chicago, 1922). 238 p., map.

    Originally published London, 1791. Repr. in Thwaites' *Early Western Travels,* II. Long was a fur trader and Indian interpreter in the old Northwest.

McCall, Hugh, *The History of Georgia . . .* (Savannah, 1811-1816). 2 vols.

    Contains much on border warfare with Creeks and Cherokees.

Marshall, Humphrey, *The History of Kentucky* . . . (Frankfort, Ky., 1824). 2 vols.

> Much on the border wars and Indian massacres.

Mather, Cotton, *Magnalia Christi Americana: or, The Ecclesiastical History of New-England, from Its First Planting in the Year 1620 unto the Year of Our Lord, 1698* (London, 1702). 8 "books" separately paged; map.

> More widely available is the Hartford edition of 1820, 2 vols. Contains much on the Indian wars of New England.

Mather, Increase, *Early History of New England; Being a Relation of Hostile Passages between the Indians and European Voyagers and First Settlers* . . . (Albany, 1864). 309 p.

> Reprint of Mather's *A Relation of the Troubles Which Have Hap'ned in New-England, by Reason of the Indians There. From the Year 1614 to the Year 1675* (Boston, 1677).

Megapolensis, Johannes, "A Short Sketch of the Mohawk Indians in New Netherland, 1644," N. Y. Hist. Soc., *Colls.*, 2d ser., 3 (1857), 137-160.

Meginness, John F., *Otzinachson; or, A History of the West Branch Valley of the Susquehanna* . . . (Phila., 1857). 518 p., illus.

Penhallow, Samuel, *The History of the Wars of New-England with the Eastern Indians* [1703-1726], N. H. Hist. Soc., *Colls.*, 1 (Concord, 1824), 13-133.

> 1st edn. Boston, 1726; repr. Cincinnati, 1859. "The chief English authority for Queen Anne's and Lovewell's wars" (Winsor).

Penn, William, *His Own Account of the Lenni Lenape or Delaware Indians, 1683,* ed. Albert Cook Myers (Moylan, Penna., 1937). 107 p., illus., facsims.

> A scholarly text of Penn's *Letter to the Free Society of Traders* (first published London, 1683), with much supporting material on Penn's relations with the Indians. Other texts of this classic account of the Delawares are available in various edns. of Penn's writings, in Myers' *Narratives of Early Pennsylvania . . . (Original Narratives of Early Amer. Hist.),* and in Old South Leaflets, No. 171).

Pouchot, M., *Memoir upon the Late War in North America, between the French and English, 1755-60,* trans. and ed. Franklin B. Hough (Roxbury, Mass., 1866). 2 vols.

Pownall, Thomas, *A Topographical Description of the Dominions of the United States of America,* ed. Lois Mulkearn (Pittsburgh, 1949). 235 p., map, facsims., bibliog.

A rev. and enl. edn. of *A Topographical Description of Such Parts of North America as Are Contained in the (Annexed) Map of the Middle British Colonies, &c. in North America,* orig. pubd. London, 1776. Pownall revised his account in 1784, but the revision remained unpublished until Mrs. Mulkearn's edition. Contains Lewis Evans' map of the Middle Colonies, and a long documentary appendix with journals of Harry Gordon, Lewis Evans, and Christopher Gist.

Rogers, Robert, *A Concise Account of North America: Containing a Description of the Several British Colonies on That Continent. . . . Also of the Interior, or Westerly Parts of the Country, upon the Rivers St. Laurence, the Mississippi, Christino, and the Great Lakes. To Which Is Subjoined, an Account of the Several Nations and Tribes of Indians Residing in Those Parts . . .* (London, 1765). 264 p.

Rogers, Robert, *Journals of Major Robert Rogers: Containing an Account of the Several Excursions He Made under the Generals Who Commanded upon the Continent of North America, during the Late War* (London, 1765). 236 p.

Covers the years 1755-1760 in the career of a celebrated border captain.

Romans, Bernard, *A Concise Natural History of East and West Florida* (N. Y., 1775). 342 p., maps, illus.

Sagard-Théodat, Gabriel, *Le Grand Voyage du Pays des Hurons* (Paris, 1632).

Repr. Paris, 1865. Repr. 1939 by Champlain Soc., Toronto, *Pubns.,* Vol. XXV, 411 p., maps, illus., as *The Long Journey to the Country of the Hurons, by Father Gabriel Sagard,* ed. George M. Wrong and trans. H. H. Langton.

Sargent, Winthrop, ed., *The History of an Expedition against Fort du Quesne, in 1755, under Major General Edward Braddock* (Phila., 1855). 423 p., maps, illus.

Introductory monograph is followed by journals of the expedition and other documents.

Simms, William Gilmore, *The History of South Carolina, from Its First European Discovery, to Its Erection into a Republic* (Charleston, 1840). 355 p.

> New edn., N. Y., 1860.

Smith, John, *Works, 1608-1631,* ed. Edward Arber (Birmingham, England, 1884). 2 vols., maps, illus.

> Rev. edn., ed. A. G. Bradley, Edinburgh, 1910.
>
> Smith's descriptions of the Tidewater Virginia Indians are the most detailed and reliable of all early accounts because they were made from his own observation and include Indian government, economy, social organization, and culture, as well as Indian-white relations for the period 1607-1624. Especially valuable are: *A True Relation of . . . Occurrences . . . in Virginia . . . ,* 1608; *A Map of Virginia . . . ,* 1612, largely a compilation from the writings of others; *The Generall Historie of Virginia, New England and the Summer Isles,* 1624, containing Hariot's description of the Roanoke Island natives and an expanded treatment of his own earlier accounts of Virginia Indians—notably the addition of the Pocahontas story.

[Smith, William], *An Historical Account of the Expedition against the Ohio Indians, in the Year 1764, under the Command of Henry Bouquet . . .* (Phila., 1765). 71 p., map, illus.

Stith, William, *History of the First Discovery and Settlement of Virginia . . .* (N. Y., 1865). 331, 34 p.

> First published Williamsburg, 1747; another edn., London, 1753.

Sullivan, James, *History of the District of Maine (1604-1795)* (Boston, 1795). 421 p., map.

Timberlake, Henry, *Lieut. Henry Timberlake's Memoirs, 1756-1765,* ed. Samuel Cole Williams (Johnson City, Tenn., 1927). 197 p., map, illus., bibliog.

> First published London, 1765; another reprint was issued at Marietta, Ga., 1948. Important data on the Cherokees and on the French and Indian war in the South.

Williams, Roger, *A Key into the Language of America: or, An help to the Language of the Natives in that part of America, called New-England. Together, with briefe Observations of the Customes,*

Manners and Worships, etc. of the aforesaid Natives, in Peace and Warre, in Life and Death . . . (London, 1643). 197 p.

Repr. in R. I. Hist. Soc., *Colls.,* 1 (1827), 17-163; also as a separate; and, authoritatively edited by J. H. Trumbull, in Narragansett Club, *Pubns.,* 1st ser., 1 (1866), 1-219. A later edition, edited by Howard M. Chapin, was published in Providence for The Rhode Island and Providence Plantations Tercentenary Committee, Inc., in 1936. Perry Miller asserts that Roger Williams was "the only Englishman of his generation" who "could treat Indian culture with respect" and that his *Key* was "the nearest approach to an objective, anthropological study that anyone was to achieve in America for a century or more" *(Roger Williams: His Contribution to the American Tradition,* Indianapolis and N. Y., 1953, pp. 52-53).

Williams, Samuel, *The Natural and Civil History of Vermont* (Burlington, 1809). 2 vols., map.

First published 1794.

Withers, Alexander S., *Chronicles of Border Warfare, or, a History of the Settlement by the Whites, of North-Western Virginia, and of the Indian Wars and Massacres in That Section of the State* . . . (Clarksburg, Va., 1831). 319 p.

New edn., Cincinnati, 1895, ed. R. G. Thwaites.

Zeisberger, David, [1721-1808], *David Zeisberger's History of Northern American Indians,* ed. Archer B. Hulbert and William N. Schwarze, Ohio Archaeol. and Hist. Soc., *Quart.,* 19 (Columbus, 1910). 189 p.

B. After 1850

Alvord, Clarence W., *The Mississippi Valley in British Politics: A Study of the Trade, Land Speculation, and Experiments in Imperialism Culminating in the American Revolution* (Cleveland, 1917). 2 vols., maps, bibliog.

Bailey, Alfred Goldsworthy, *The Conflict of European and Eastern Algonkian Cultures, 1504-1700,* New Brunswick Mus., *Pubns., Monograph Ser.,* No. 2 (St. John, 1937). 206 p., bibliog.

A most important if little-known analysis of historical sources from an ethnological point of view.

Baker-Crothers, Hayes, *Virginia and the French and Indian War* (Chicago, 1928). 179 p., bibliog.

Barnhart, John D., *Henry Hamilton and George Rogers Clark in the American Revolution, with the Unpublished Journal of Lieut. Gov. Henry Hamilton* (Crawfordsville, Ind., 1951). 244 p.

Hamilton commanded the Indians loyal to England in the Great Lakes region during the Revolution and had an unsavory reputation in Virginia.

Beauchamp, William M., *A History of the New York Iroquois, Now Commonly Called the Six Nations,* N. Y. State Mus., *Bull.* 78 (Albany, 1905), 126-461, maps, illus.

Beauchamp's history documents the intense official interest in the Iroquois from early times. Published by the State Education Department as a State Museum Bull., it has long been out-of-print and sadly needs replacement by a more comprehensive political history of the Six Nations, written from historical and ethnological sources.

Bond, Richmond P., *Queen Anne's American Kings* (Oxford, 1952). 148 p., illus.

Definitive study of the political, literary, and other aspects of the visit by three Iroquois chiefs and one Mahican sachem to the court of Queen Anne in 1710.

Bradshaw, Harold C., *The Indians of Connecticut; the Effect of English Colonization and of Missionary Activity on Indian Life in Connecticut* (Deep River, Conn., 1935). 64 p., bibliog.

Brown, John P., *Old Frontiers: The Story of the Cherokee Indians from Earliest Times to the Date of Their Removal to the West, 1838* (Kingsport, Tenn., 1938). 570 p., maps, illus., bibliog.

Collier, John, *The Indians of the Americas* (N. Y., 1947). 326 p., maps, illus., bibliog.

Corry, John P., *Indian Affairs in Georgia, 1732-1756* (Phila., 1936). 197 p., maps, bibliog.

Cotterill, R. S., *The Southern Indians: The Story of the Civilized Tribes before Removal* (Norman, Okla., 1954). 255 p., maps, illus., bibliog.

Crane, Verner W., *The Southern Frontier, 1670-1732* (Durham, N. C., 1928). 391 p., map, bibliog.

Debo, Angie, *The Road to Disappearance* (Norman, Okla., 1941). 399 p., maps, illus., bibliog.

History of the Creek confederacy from before white contact until the present day.

DeForest, John W., *History of the Indians of Connecticut from the Earliest Known Period to 1850* (Hartford, 1851). 509 p., map, illus.
Written by an undergraduate at Yale College, it remains the best general account.

De Haas, Wills, *History of the Early Settlement and Indian Wars of Western Virginia, Embracing an Account of the Various Expeditions in the West, Previous to 1795* . . . (Wheeling, 1851). 416 p.

Downes, Randolph C., *Council Fires on the Upper Ohio: A Narrative of Indian Affairs in the Upper Ohio Valley until 1795* (Pittsburgh, 1940). 367 p., map, bibliog.

Drake, Samuel G., *A Particular History of the Five Years French and Indian War in New England and Parts Adjacent* . . . (Boston, 1870). 312 p.
Useful for its documents.

Ellis, George E., *The Red Man and the White Man in North America, from Its Discovery to the Present Time* (Boston, 1882). 642 p.
A comprehensive and sensible treatise but without documentation.

Ellis, George W., and John E. Morris, *King Philip's War* . . . *with Biographical and Topographical Notes* (N. Y., 1906). 326 p., illus.
An authoritative brief account, with photographs of the sites of events of the war.

Eshleman, H. Frank, *Lancaster County Indians: Annals of the Susquehannocks and Other Indian Tribes of the Susquehanna Territory from about the Year 1500 to 1763* (Lancaster, Penna., 1909). 415 p.
A useful but not well-balanced compendium.

Evans, George Hill, *Pigwacket* (Conway, N. H., 1939), 135 p., map, bibliog.
N. H. Hist. Soc., Pubn. No. 1. Has a good bibliog. on the Indians of Maine, pp. 127-135.

Fairbanks, George R., *History of Florida* . . . *1512-1842* (Phila. and Jacksonville, 1871). 350 p.

Foreman, Carolyn Thomas, *Indians Abroad, 1493-1938* (Norman, Okla., 1943). 247 p., illus., bibliog.
This is an excellent introduction to a fascinating topic, but more work remains to be done on this theme. For a definitive study of a

visit of four Indian leaders to England, see the reference to Bond in this section.

Foreman, Grant, *Indians and Pioneers: The Story of the American Southwest before 1830* (New Haven, 1930). 348 p., map, illus., bibliog.

Revised edn., Norman, 1936.

Gabriel, Ralph Henry, *The Lure of the Frontier: A Story of Race Conflict* (New Haven, 1929). 327 p., illus.

Vol. II in *The Pageant of America.*

Gipson, Lawrence Henry, *The Great War for Empire* [1754-1763], Vols. VI, VII, VIII, of *The British Empire before the American Revolution* (N. Y., 1946-1954).

Vol. IX: *The Triumphant Empire* (N. Y., 1956), gives emphasis to North American Indian relations, including two great Indian wars covering the period from 1759 to 1764.

Glenn, Keith, "Captain John Smith and the Indians," *Va. Mag. Hist. and Biog.,* 52 (1944), 228-248.

Halbert, Henry S., and T. H. Ball, *The Creek War of 1813 and 1814* (Chicago and Montgomery, 1895). 331 p., illus., maps.

Halsey, Francis W., *The Old New York Frontier, ... 1614-1800* (N. Y., 1901). 432 p., maps, illus.

Hanna, Charles A., *The Wilderness Trail, or The Ventures and Adventures of the Pennsylvania Traders on the Allegheny Path* (N. Y., 1911). 2 vols., maps, illus.

Deals with the Indian tribes and leaders and their relations with the whites in the first half of the 18th century from the Susquehanna to Kentucky. Chapters on the Iroquois in Pennsylvania, Delaware, Shawnee, Andrew Montour, routes of the traders in Pennsylvania and Ohio, Ohio Mingoes, George Croghan, John Finley in Kentucky, etc. Data on Indian villages. Many maps and illustrations. Many documents quoted *in extenso.* Footnote citations but no bibliography.

Harvey, Henry, *History of the Shawnee Indians, from the Year 1681 to 1854* (Cincinnati, 1855). 316 p.

Regarded by modern ethnologists as a valuable work because the author, a Quaker, wrote from first-hand knowledge.

Hulbert, Archer B., *Indian Thoroughfares* (Cleveland, 1902). 152 p., maps, illus.

Historic Highways of America, II. Relates principally to the Northeast and the earliest Northwest.

Hunt, George T., *The Wars of the Iroquois: A Study in Intertribal Trade Relations* (Madison, Wis., 1940). 209 p., map, bibliog.

The discussion of earlier historical treatment of the Iroquois and their League at the beginning of the bibliography is stimulating and iconoclastic.

Jacobs, Wilbur R., *Diplomacy and Indian Gifts: Anglo-French Rivalry along the Ohio and Northwest Frontiers, 1748-1763* (Stanford, Calif., 1950). 208 p., map, illus.

James, James A., *English Institutions and the American Indian* (Baltimore, 1894). 59 p.

Jones, Charles Colcock, *Antiquities of the Southern Indians, Particularly of the Georgia Tribes* (N. Y., 1873). 532 p., illus.

Kellogg, Louise Phelps, *The British Régime in Wisconsin and the Northwest* (Madison, Wis., 1935). 361 p., maps, illus.

Kellogg, Louise Phelps, *The French Régime in Wisconsin and the Northwest* (Madison, Wis., 1925). 474 p., maps, illus.

Ketchum, William, *An Authentic and Comprehensive History of Buffalo, with Some Account of Its Early Inhabitants, Both Savage and Civilized* ... (Buffalo, 1864-1865). 2 vols.

Devotes a great deal of space to Indian affairs in western New York, reprinting Kirkland's journal and similar documents.

Lauber, Almon W., *Indian Slavery in Colonial Times within the Present Limits of the United States* (N. Y., 1913). 352 p., bibliog.

Marshall, Orsamus H., *Historical Writings ... Relating to the Early History of the West* (Albany, 1887). 500 p., maps.

Relates especially to western New York and the French period in Canada.

McCary, Ben Clyde, *Indians in Seventeenth-Century Virginia,* Virginia 350th Anniversary Historical Booklet, No. 18 (Williamsburg, 1957). 93 p., bibliog.

McNickle, D'Arcy, *They Came Here First: The Epic of the American Indian* (Phila., 1949). 325 p., "Source Notes."

A brilliant short study, combining the ethnological and historical approaches.

Mayer, Brantz, *Tah-Gah-Jute; or, Logan and Cresap, an Historical Essay* (Albany, 1867). 204 p.

A study of the controversy arising from the murder of the family of Logan, a Mingo chief on the upper Ohio, in 1774. The incident had been given wide currency by Jefferson's printing of Logan's speech to Lord Dunmore in his *Notes on the State of Virginia.* Mayer attacks Jefferson's account.

Milling, Chapman J., *Red Carolinians* (Chapel Hill, 1940). 438 p., illus., bibliog.

An authoritative account of the Indians and of Indian-white relations in South Carolina.

Moloney, Francis Xavier, *The Fur Trade in New England, 1620-1676* (Cambridge, Mass., 1931). 150 p.

Myer, William E., *Indian Trails of the Southeast,* Bur. Amer. Ethnol., 42d *Ann. Report,* 1924-1925 (Wash., 1928), 727-857, maps, bibliog.

Nelson, William, *The Indians of New Jersey* (Paterson, N. J., 1894). 168 p.

Parkman, Francis, *History of the Conspiracy of Pontiac, and the War of the North American Tribes against the English Colonies after the Conquest of Canada* (Boston, 1851). 630 p., maps.

This is the 1st edition of Parkman's classic work, later revised and issued under the title *The Conspiracy of Pontiac.* There is an initial chapter on "Indian Tribes East of the Mississippi." The work is not part of, but is closely connected with, the sequence of seven historical narratives that Parkman published under the collective title, "France and England in North America" (Boston, 1865-1892), as follows: *Pioneers of France in the New World, The Jesuits in North America, LaSalle and the Discovery of the Great West, The Old Regime in Canada, Count Frontenac and New France, A Half-Century of Conflict,* and *Montcalm and Wolfe.* All of these are concerned in greater or less degree with Indian relations in North America, especially the northeastern region. For important materials on Parkman's aims and methods of work as a historian, see Mason Wade, ed., *The Journals of Francis Parkman* (N. Y., 1947). 2 vols.

An edition of Parkman's letters, from originals in the Massachusetts Historical Society and other sources, is in preparation by Wilbur R. Jacobs.

Pennsylvania Commission to Locate the Site of the Frontier Forts, *Report* ([Harrisburg], 1896). 2 vols., map, illus.

Report of Commission established by an act of 1893 to locate and mark sites of "the various forts erected as a defense against the Indians by the early settlers of this Commonwealth" prior to 1783. The State was divided into five districts for this purpose, and each member of the Commission was responsible for his district. The *Report* is chiefly remarkable for the detailed plans (in color in the first edition) of every fort located; it also contains an immense mass of documents and lore relating to early Indian-white relations.

Pickett, Albert James, *History of Alabama, and Incidentally of Georgia and Mississippi, from the Earliest Period* [to 1819] (Charleston, 1851). 2 vols., illus., maps.

Several later editions. An important pioneer history with much firsthand information on the Indians of the region.

Radin, Paul, *The Story of the American Indian* (N. Y., 1927). 371 p., illus.

Revised edn. 1934 with bibliog.; repr. 1937.

Not always reliable historically, Radin had brilliant insights, a nice sense of problem, and his own published field studies of Ojibwa and Winnebago religious life show a deep understanding of Indians as human beings. See particularly *The Winnebago Tribe* (1923); *Crashing Thunder,* an autobiography (1926); *Primitive Man as Philosopher* (1927); *The Method and Theory of Ethnology* (1933).

Reynolds, John, *The Pioneer History of Illinois, 1673-1818* (Chicago, 1887). 459 p., illus.

First published in Belleville, Ill., 1852.

Rights, Douglas L., *The American Indian in North Carolina* (Durham, 1947). 296 p., maps, illus.

Contains much local history and local archeology, on which the author is the primary authority, and reprints historical sources like Lawson; but the method is not critical, either historically or ethnologically.

Riley, Franklin L., "Choctaw Land Claims," Mississippi Hist. Soc., *Pubns.,* 8 (Oxford, 1904), 345-395.

Story of the Choctaw Land Fraud, 1830-1846. This volume of Mississippi Hist. Soc. *Pubns.* contains numerous other articles on the Choctaws and Chickasaws, including "The Removal of the Mississippi Choctaws," by John William Wade, pp. 397-426.

Royce, Charles C., *The Cherokee Nation of Indians,* Bur. Amer.
Ethnol., 5th *Ann. Report,* 1883-1884 (Wash., 1887), 121-378, maps.
"The earliest authoritative history of the Cherokees, based pri-
marily on a painstaking analysis of government documents"
(Starkey, *Cherokee Nation*).

Ruttenber, Edward M., *History of the Indian Tribes of Hudson's River*
... (Albany, 1872). 415 p., illus.
This scarce book contains much original material on the Algon-
quian-speaking Mahican Indians of Hudson's River nowhere else
available.

Scheele, Raymond, *Warfare of the Iroquois and their Northern Neighbors* (Ann Arbor: University Microfilms Pubn. No. 2128, 1950
[i.e., 1951]). 149 p.

Schoolcraft, Henry R., *Historical and Statistical Information, respecting the History, Condition and Prospects of the Indian Tribes of
the United States* ... (Phila., 1851-1857). 6 vols., illus.
An *Index to Schoolcraft's "Indian Tribes of the United States"*
has been compiled by Frances S. Nichols, Bur. Amer. Ethnol., *Bull.*
152 (Wash., 1954). A bibliography of Schoolcraft is contained in
Chase S. and Stellanova Osborn, *Schoolcraft, Longfellow, Hiawatha* (Lancaster, Pa., 1942), pp. 624-653.

Semmes, Raphael, "Aboriginal Maryland, 1608-1689," *Md. Hist. Mag.,*
24 (1929), 157-172, 195-209.

Severance, Frank H., *An Old Frontier of France: The Niagara Region
and Adjacent Lakes under French Control* (N. Y., 1917). 2 vols.,
maps, illus.

Shea, John Gilmary, *Discovery and Exploration of the Mississippi
Valley* (2d edn., Albany, 1903). 267 p., maps., illus.
1st published N. Y., 1852.

Sheldon, George, ... *A History of Deerfield, Massachusetts ... with a
Special Study of the Indian Wars in the Connecticut Valley* (Deerfield, 1895-1896). 2 vols., illus.
A scholarly work important for the history of Indian contacts
and for John Pynchon's activities, but heavily biased against the
aborigines.

Sipe, Chester Hale, *The Indian Wars of Pennsylvania: An Account of
the Indian Events, in Pennsylvania, of the French and Indian War,*

Pontiac's War, Lord Dunmore's War, the Revolutionary War and the Indian Uprising from 1789 to 1795 (Harrisburg, 1929). 793 p. Undocumented mélange.

Smith, Robinson V., "New Hampshire Remembers the Indians," *Historical New Hampshire*, 8, No. 2 (1952). 36 p.

A brief sketch of Indian-white relations in New Hampshire in the colonial period. Contains numerous illustrations taken from collections in the New Hampshire Historical Society.

Spiess, Mathias, *The Indians of Connecticut*, Conn. Tercentenary Commission, Pamphlet XIX (New Haven, 1933). 33 p.

Starkey, Marion L., *The Cherokee Nation* (N. Y., 1946). 355 p., map, illus., facsims.

Story of the removal of the Cherokees, with the causes and consequences of the removal in relation to public opinion and American history generally. Uses valuable papers and broadsides of the American Board of Commissioners for Foreign Missions, Boston, in Houghton Library, Harvard University.

Swiggett, Howard, *War Out of Niagara: Walter Butler and the Tory Rangers* (N. Y., 1933). 309 p., illus., bibliog.

The best study of Tory-Indian guerrilla warfare on the New York-Pennsylvania frontier during the Revolution.

Sylvester, Herbert Milton, *Indian Wars of New England* (Boston, 1910). 3 vols.

An exhaustive and tedious narrative, based on the sources, many of which are here printed or paraphrased at length.

Trumbull, J. Hammond, "The Composition of Indian Geographical Names, Illustrated from the Algonkin Languages," Connecticut Hist. Soc., *Collections*, 2 (Hartford, 1870), 1-50.

Underhill, Ruth Murray, *Red Man's America: A History of the Indians in the United States* (Chicago, 1953). 400 p., maps, illus., bibliog.

Weeden, William B., "Indian Money as a Factor in New England Civilization," Johns Hopkins Univ., *Studies in Hist. and Pol. Sci.*, 2d ser., 8-9 (Baltimore, 1884), 1-51.

Whitaker, Arthur P., *The Spanish-American Frontier, 1783-1795* (Boston, 1927). 255 p., maps.

Williams, Samuel Cole, *Beginnings of West Tennessee: In the Land of the Chickasaws, 1541-1841* (Johnson City, Tenn., 1930). 331 p., maps, facsim., bibliog.

Williams, Samuel Cole, *Dawn of Tennessee Valley and Tennessee History* (Johnson City, Tenn., 1937). 495 p., maps, bibliog.

   Contains much on early white contact with Cherokees and Chickasaws.

Willson, Minnie Moore, *The Seminoles of Florida* (Phila., 1896). 126 p., illus.

   Second edn., N. Y., 1910. 213 p.

PART IV

SERIALS

In a selective bibliography such as this, only a few of the more significant and more unusual serials can be listed. The student should be aware, however, of the most comprehensive guide to serials, the *Union List of Serials in Libraries of the United States and Canada* (2d edn., N. Y., 1943), with supplements. For older journals, some of which are important for the student of Indian-white relations, see Justin Winsor, *Narrative and Critical History,* I, 437-444. See *Harvard Guide to American History,* pp. 163-170, for lists of national, regional, state, local, university, and society serials. Historical society serials are indexed to 1905 in Appleton Prentiss Clark Griffin's *Bibliography of American Historical Societies (The United States and the Dominion of Canada)*, Amer. Hist. Assoc., *Ann. Report,* 1905, II (Wash., 1907), 1-1374. A handy guide for the student is the *Directory of Historical Societies and Agencies in the United States and Canada, 1956,* issued by the American Association for State and Local History (Columbus, O., 1956), 48 p.

Alabama Anthropological Society. Montgomery. *Arrow Points,* 1920-1937.
American *Anthropologist.* Wash., 1888-1898; new ser., 1899-   .
    Index to 1888-1928 in Vol. 32; to 1929-1938 in Vol. 42.
American Antiquarian Society. Worcester, Mass. *Archaeologia Americana (Transactions and Collections),* 1820-1885. *Proceedings,* 1843-   .
American Antiquity: A Quarterly Review of American Archaeology. Menasha, Wis., 1935-   .
American Museum of Natural History. N. Y. *Bulletin,* 1881-   . *Anthropological Papers,* 1907-   .
American Philosophical Society. Phila., *Transactions,* 1769-1809; new ser., 1818-   . *Proceedings,* 1838-   .
    Indexes have been published to the *Procs.,* 1838-1911, 1912-1935.
Archeological Society of Delaware. Wilmington. *Bulletin,* 1933-   . *Papers,* 1939-   .
Canada. National Museum. Ottawa. *Museum Bulletin,* 1913-   .

The bulletins are numbered consecutively and are also divided into three subseries: Geological series, Biological series, and Anthropological series, each with its own numbering: Bull. No. 1 contains Geological series No. 1-12, Biological series No. 1-3, and Anthropological series No. 1; Bull. No. 2 contains Geological series No. 13-18, Anthropological series No. 2. Beginning with No. 3 the bulletins are issued as monographs. Title varies: No. 1, Victoria Memorial Museum Bulletin; Nos. 2-31, 40-41, 43, 45, Museum Bulletin; Nos. 32-39, 42, 44, 46-47, 49-   , Bulletin.

Ethnohistory. Bloomington, Ind., 1954-   .

A quarterly journal devoted to "original research in the documentary history of the culture and movements of primitive peoples," and sponsored by the American Indian Ethnohistoric Conference (formerly the Ohio Valley Historic Indian Conference).

Explorations: Studies in Culture and Communication. Toronto, 1953-   .

Field Museum of Natural History. Chicago. *Publications,* 1894-   . *Anthropological Series,* 1895-   .

Harvard University. Peabody Museum of American Archaeology and Ethnology. Cambridge. *Papers,* 1888-   . *Memoirs,* 1896-   .

Heye Foundation. Museum of the American Indian. N. Y. *Contributions,* 1913-   . *Indian Notes and Monographs,* 1919-   .

Ohio Historical Society. Columbus. *Ohio State Archaeological and Historical Quarterly,* 1887-1954. *Ohio Historical Quarterly,* 1955-   .

Journal of American Folklore. Phila., 1888-   .

Index to Vols. 1-40.

New York State Museum. Albany. *Bulletin,* 1887-   .

Only certain of these deal with archeology, but those that do include important contributions by Beauchamp, Parker, and others.

Pennsylvania Magazine of History and Biography. Phila., 1877-   .

The files of this magazine have been rendered eminently usable by the excellent *Index* to Vols. 1-75 (1877-1951) ed. Eugene E. Doll (Phila., 1954).

U. S. Bureau of American Ethnology. Washington, D. C. *Contributions to North American Ethnology,* 1877-1895. *Miscellaneous Publications,* 1880-   . *Annual Reports,* 1881-   . *Bulletins,* 1887-   .

See *List of Publications of the Bureau of American Ethnology...
Revised to July 30, 1949* (Wash., 1949).

Wenner-Gren Foundation for Anthropological Research. N. Y. *Viking
Fund Publications in Anthropology,* 1943-   .

Yale University. *Publications in Anthropology,* 1936-   .

PART V

MANUSCRIPT SOURCES

Manuscript materials relating to the Indians in North America east of the Mississippi will be found in all the major libraries and archival repositories in that area, in many lesser ones, and in certain research libraries and archives elsewhere in the United States and abroad. The following data, arranged according to geographical regions, are therefore highly selective and intended to be merely suggestive.

The searcher for MSS on this subject has a useful aid in the form of Ray A. Billington, "Guides to American History Manuscript Collections in Libraries of the United States," *Miss. Valley Hist. Rev.,* 38 (1951), 467-496 (also issued separately, N. Y., 1952), which lists such guides as have been published and may therefore be consulted in any adequate library. A similar listing is given in the *Harvard Guide,* pp. 79-87. Both include the major pertinent publications of the Historical Records Survey in the 1930's, of which, unfortunately, there is no complete and reliable list in print. Two aids to research that are now in progress will eventually be of very great service to those wishing to discover where pertinent manuscript sources are. One of these is a "Guide to Depositories of Historical Manuscripts in the United States," being compiled for publication in 1957 by the National Historical Publications Commission at the National Archives. The other is a National Register of Manuscript Collections, now far along in the planning stage at the Library of Congress and intended to correspond in form and coverage, so far as possible, with the National Union Catalog of printed materials held by U. S. libraries.

For guidance to foreign archives and manuscript collections, see the discussion and lists in the *Harvard Guide,* pp. 87-88, which include the notable series of "Carnegie Guides" to materials for American history compiled and published from 1907 onward by the Carnegie Institution of Washington. Most important for Indian relations to 1830 are, of course, the Carnegie publications covering British, French, Spanish, Canadian, and Mexican archives.

Writers of monographs sometimes provide very full lists and critical discussions of the manuscript sources they have used. Examples are the monographs of Annie H. Abel, John R. Alden, Grant Foreman, and George D. Harmon listed elsewhere in the present bibliography. Attention is also called to two articles that are bibliographical in character:

Fenton, William N., "A Calendar of Manuscript Materials Relating to the History of the Six Nations or Iroquois in Depositories Outside of Philadelphia," 1750-1850, Amer. Philos. Soc., *Procs.*, 97 (1953), 578-595.

Snyderman, George S., "Preliminary Survey of American Indian Manuscripts in Repositories of the Philadelphia Area," Amer. Philos. Soc., *Procs.*, 97 (1953), 596-610.

New England

At Dartmouth College are the extensive Eleazar Wheelock Papers relating to Wheelock's Indian School and missionary activities in New England and New York. These include letters of Indians to Wheelock and his colleagues. Important segments of the Wheelock Papers have been published in the Dartmouth College Publications listed elsewhere in this bibliography (see § VII, E). In the Massachusetts Historical Society, Boston, are the Knox, Pickering, Parkman, and Winthrop Papers, among others. All are important for the subject of Indian relations; see the Society's *Handbook* (Boston, 1948). Harvard College Library has the Papers of the American Board of Commissioners for Foreign Missions, which document missionary work among the Indians.

In the State House in Boston the Massachusetts Archives, the colonial portions of which are arranged by subject, contain six volumes on "Indians" (Vols. 29-34). Other Indian material can be found in the volumes labeled "Military," "Lands," "Letters," etc. Some of this material has been printed in the publications of the various New England historical societies, but much has never been published.

In Salem, at the Essex Institute, are additional Pickering Papers documenting the career of the noted Indian negotiator Timothy Pickering. In Worcester, at the American Antiquarian Society, is an extensive and important collection of manuscripts relating to the French and Indian War.

Little use has been made of the county court and other local records in New England, yet some county records, for example, those of Plymouth and Bristol in Massachusetts, contain much information on Indian-white relations. Still a useful guide to the Massachusetts local records is Carroll D. Wright, *Report on the Custody and Condition of the Public Records of Parishes, Towns, and Counties* (Boston, 1889). Thirty-one succeeding *Reports* of the Massachusetts Commissioner of Public Records, 1888-1919, were published (Boston, 1889-1920).

Middle Atlantic States

In the New York State Library at Albany is the great collection of Sir William Johnson Papers, both originals and transcripts; these are being definitively edited by the State. Also in upper New York State, in the Hamilton College Library at Clinton, are the diaries, correspondence, and other papers of Samuel Kirkland, the founder of Hamilton College and missionary to the Senecas and Oneidas. Walter Pilkington, the librarian, has in preparation a biography of Kirkland, which has long been a desideratum of Indian studies. Much Indian material is referenced in the *Guide to Depositories of Manuscript Collections in New York State (Exclusive of New York City)*, prepared by the Historical Records Survey of the Works Projects Administration (Albany and Cooperstown, 1941-1944), 2 vols.

In New York City the Philip Schuyler Papers and George Chalmers Collection in the New York Public Library touch on Indian affairs at many points. At the New-York Historical Society the following collections are especially pertinent: Colden Papers, French and Indian War Collections, Gallatin Papers (include much material on Indian languages), Gates Papers, Indian Collection, Horsmanden Papers, McKesson Papers, and O'Reilly Papers (15 vols. on the Indians of western New York). For a detailed guide, see Evarts B. Greene and Richard B. Morris, *A Guide to the Principal Sources for Early American History (1600-1800) in the City of New York*, 2d edn., revised by Richard B. Morris (N. Y., 1953).

Several repositories in Philadelphia are extremely rich for the student of Indian history. They are all treated in Snyderman's article cited above. The Historical Society of Pennsylvania's *Guide to the Manuscript Collections* (2d edn., 1949) is a key to its extensive holdings, which include the important diaries of George Croghan, John Parrish, and Christian Post, Timothy Horsfield's letterbook, an Indian Records Collection, and the Henry, Irvine, Logan, Daniel Parker, Pemberton, Penn, Peters, Shippen Family, Trent, Wayne, and Weiser Papers.

The American Philosophical Society was an early center for research on the American Indian (see Wissler's article in § II) and has important holdings on Indian linguistics and Indian history which it is actively expanding and supplementing by the acquisition of photocopies as well as original materials, including the papers of eminent ethnologists. C. F. Voegelin and Z. S. Harris have compiled an *Index to the Franz Boas Collection of Materials for American Linguistics* in the American Philosophical Society Library; Linguistic Society of America, *Language Monographs,* No. 22 (Balt., 1945).

Elsewhere in Pennsylvania, besides the public records of the State in Harrisburg, the Archives of the Moravian Church, at Bethlehem, deserve particular mention because they include records of the Moravian Society for Propagating the Gospel among the Heathen, 1735-1811, and personal papers of such figures as David Zeisberger and John Heckewelder. Paul A. W. Wallace discusses these figures in "They Knew the Indian: The Men Who Wrote the Moravian Records," Amer. Philos. Soc., *Procs.,* 95 (1951), 290-295. The Indian MS material of the Moravian Church fills about seventy cartons, all of which are indexed.

District of Columbia

The main body of federal records relating directly to Indians is in the National Archives Record Group 75, Records of the Office of Indian Affairs. RG 75 includes the records of the agencies antecedent to the Office of Indian Affairs, as well as the files of that office, which was a part of the War Department until 1849 when it was transfered to the newly-established Interior Department. See *Guide to the Records in the National Archives* (Wash., 1948), pp. 295-303. Important segments of RG 75 have been published on microfilm, e.g., Letters Sent by the Secretary of War, Indian Affairs, 1800-1824; and Letters Sent by the Superintendent of Indian Trade, 1807-1823; see *List of National Archives Microfilm Publications* (Wash., 1953), pp. 62-67. Gaston Litton's "The Resources of the National Archives for the Study of the American Indian," published in *Ethnohistory,* 2 (1955), 191-208, is an excellent general introduction for the inquiring researcher. The National Archives' *List of Documents Concerning the Negotiation of Ratified Indian Treaties, 1801-1869* (*Special List* No. 6, Washington, 1949, 175 p.), includes material from both RG 75 and RG 48 (General Records of the Department of the Interior) and appends a valuable list of federal officials concerned in negotiating Indian treaties.

The constitutional control exercised by the Congress of the United States over Indian affairs since 1789 is heavily reflected in National Archives Record Group 46, Records of the United States Senate, and Record Group 233, Records of the United States House of Representatives. The nature of much of what is available can be deduced from the numerous items that have been published in the *American State Papers* and in the many thousands of volumes comprising the Congressional Series of publications. The printed journals of the respective houses key their proceedings; and from the printed journals in any large library the serious student can compile a reasonably good list of the specific documentary items that he may wish produced at the National Archives from the original files. *A Preliminary Inventory of the Records of the United States Senate,* by Harold E. Hufford and Watson G. Caudill, was processed in 1950; and Harold E. Hufford and Buford Rowland are now putting the finishing touches on a similar inventory of the original records of the United States House of Representatives.

Other Indian material which should not be overlooked is contained among the papers of the General Accounting Office. Though dealing mainly with the financial aspects of the operations of Indian superintendents, agents, and subagents, this material contains many supporting documents, including correspondence, which are almost indispensable in any study of Indian relations. This Indian material is to be found in a separate file maintained by the General Accounting Office, and in the main General Accounting Office file in the National Archives.

Some early maps relating to Indian tribes and treaties are listed in Laura E. Kelsay, comp., *List of Cartographic Records of the Bureau of Indian Affairs,* National Archives, *Special List* No. 13 (Wash., 1954).

For Indian affairs during the Revolutionary and Confederation period, 1774-1789, the Papers of the Continental Congress, transferred from the Library of Congress to the National Archives in 1952, are basic. Unfortunately there is no satisfactory catalogue of this extensive body of records. A convenient but partial listing of the nearly 200 series into which they were arbitrarily arranged by State Department clerks over a century ago is in the Library of Congress, *Handbook of Manuscripts* (Wash., 1918), pp. 79-90; somewhat more complete is a *Catalogue of the Papers of the Continental Congress,* Dept. of State, Bur. of Rolls and Libr., *Bull.* No. 1 (Wash., 1893). Indian affairs bulk large in many parts of the P.C.C., but note especially the following series: No. 30, Reports of Committees on Indian Affairs and Land in the Western Territory, 1776-1788; No. 56, Letters and Papers Relative to Indian Affairs, 1765-1789; No. 134, Proceedings of the Committee Appointed to Treat with the Six Nations of Indians, 1775; No. 166, Letters and Papers Relative to Canadian Affairs, General Sullivan's Expedition, 1779, and the Northern Indians; No. 174, Record of Indian Treaties, 1784-1786. The letters and papers of such officers as Hand, St. Clair, Schuyler, Sullivan, and Washington in P.C.C. are also of importance for this subject. It is gratifying to learn that plans for publishing the entire corpus of the P.C.C. on microfilm have now matured and the films are in production. The full history of the Indians and the American Revolution remains to be written, and these are basic records for that story.

The principal key to the vast holdings of the Manuscripts Division of the Library of Congress is its *Handbook of Manuscripts* (Wash., 1918), for which two supplements have been published, a *List . . . to July, 1931,* compiled by Curtis W. Garrison (Wash., 1932), and a further *List . . . July, 1931 to July, 1938,* compiled by C. Percy Powell (Wash., 1939). These are in turn supplemented by the *Annual Reports* of the Librarian and, since 1943, by reports and articles on manuscript additions in the Library's *Quarterly Journal of Current Acquisitions.* Following is a selection of the Library of Congress manuscript collections containing significant materials relating to Indians: Colden Papers, Hand Papers, Indians Collection, Journals and Diaries, McHenry Papers, George Morgan Papers, St. Clair Papers, Schoolcraft Papers, Adam Stephen Papers, U. S. Army, and U. S. Indian Affairs Collections. In the various collections arranged under the names of the older states of the Union are many documents relating to Indians. This is also true of the great series of Presidential Papers (especially those of Washington, Jefferson, Madison, Monroe, and Jackson) and of the papers of other statesmen and military leaders too numerous even to list here.

The Manuscripts Division of the Library of Congress preserves and services a very extensive collection of transcripts and photocopies of MSS relating to American history in foreign archives. The brief descriptions of transcripts in the *Handbook* of 1918 cover only a fraction of this collection, for the bulk has been acquired since publication of that guide. For the British transcripts there is a valuable *Guide to Manuscripts Relating to American History Reproduced for the Division of Manuscripts of the Library of Congress* by Grace Gardner Griffin (Wash., 1946).

At the Smithsonian Institution, the Bureau of American Ethnology maintains an archive containing the original field notes, maps, photographs, and unpublished manuscripts of its former staff including the Gatchet, Hewitt, Mooney, and Powell papers and other relevant materials, all well-catalogued and easily accessible to the visiting scholar.

By Public Law No. 726, 79th Cong., 2d Sess. (Aug. 13, 1946), an Indian Claims Commission, consisting of three commissioners with headquarters in Washington, was established to hear and determine claims against the United States on behalf of any Indian tribe. In the years following the enactment of this legislation numerous claims have been submitted. A great amount of historical research has been done to determine the area, period, and manner of Indian occupancy of land allegedly unjustly taken by the government, as well as to establish the facts of other matters in dispute. This research has not been localized but is being carried out simultaneously in various parts of the country by those engaged in the preparation of, or defense against, the claims. The University of Indiana, Bloomington, is one of the several places at which research is being conducted. It is expected that much of the material collected will eventually be deposited in libraries and made available to all scholars.

Not to be overlooked by the scholar working in the Washington area is the Folger Library, which, in addition to its Shakespearian materials, contains a very impressive collection of early printed books on English travel and exploration in the New World.

South

In the southern states there are several nationally known manuscript repositories containing Indian materials, including those of the University of Virginia, Duke University, and the Southern Historical Collections at the University of North Carolina. For the latter two there are published guides, and the University of Virginia issues *Annual Reports* on its historical collections. The state archival agencies and historical societies in these and the other southern states cannot be overlooked, and attention is called particularly to the unusually full 18th-century records pertaining to Indian affairs in the South Carolina Archives Department at Columbia; these will in due course be published as Series 2 of the South Carolina Colonial Records. The first volume has already been published (see South Carolina in § VI). Important groups of papers of Benjamin Hawkins, Indian agent and philanthropist, are in the Georgia Historical Society and the Georgia Department of Archives and History. The Department of Archives and History of the State of North Carolina, Raleigh, possesses papers relating to the Cherokee and Tuscarora Indians from the early eighteenth century; 10,000 photostats and typed copies of original records in the Spanish Archives, 1566-1802; the Thomas Pollock Papers, 1706-1761, containing letters relative to Indian wars as well as Pollock's official letters as governor of North Carolina; and other miscellaneous documents relating to the Indians.

Much material on the Gulf Coast areas of the United States in the early period is contained in the Cuban and Spanish archives. Documents relating to U. S. history in these archives have been calendared in various Carnegie Institution *Guides* compiled by Luis Marino Perez (Wash., 1907), James Alexander Robertson (Wash., 1910), and Roscoe R. Hill (Wash., 1916). La Sociedad Colombista Panamericana has issued *Documents Pertaining to the Floridas which are kept in Different Archives of Cuba, Appendix Number 1: Official List of Documentary Funds of The Floridas—now territories of the States of Louisiana, Alabama, Mississippi, Georgia and Florida—kept in the National Archives* (*Havana, 1945*). The interested student will find later discussions of the Spanish records at intervals in the *Hispanic American Historical Review.*

Middle West

Several repositories in this area are outstanding for their holdings relating to Indian affairs. The recent *Guide to the Manuscript Collections in the William L. Clements Library,* compiled by William S.

Ewing (Ann Arbor, 1953), lists Indian materials in its Albany Congress, Amherst, Cass, Gage, Germain, Henry Hamilton, Harmar, Robert Rogers, Shelburne, and Simcoe Papers.

The Burton Historical Collection of the Detroit Public Library has numerous papers dealing with the fur trade in the Great Lakes region in the late eighteenth and early nineteenth centuries. The Collection also contains manuscripts relating to the Indian Wars, 1790-1796, and the George Ironside Papers, comprising the correspondence and papers of the Ironsides, father and son, agents in the British Indian Department at Amherstburg and Manitowaning, Ontario, in the period 1790-1848.

Ruth Lapham Butler has compiled *A Check List of Manuscripts in the Edward E. Ayer Collection* in the Newberry Library, Chicago (Chicago, 1937). Ayer was a leading collector of Indian ethnology, linguistics, and history, and he gathered in letters and documents of Indian traders, agents, missionaries, fighters, and scholars; the papers of John Howard Payne relating to the Cherokees and other tribes constitute one important group in this large but miscellaneous collection.

The University of Chicago Library has a collection of ethnohistorical materials on Indians of the Great Lakes area collected, microfilmed, and calendared mainly by Sarah Jones Tucker.

The Ohio Historical Society in Columbus has the papers of Warren King Moorehead (1866-1939), pioneer Ohio archeologist whose interest in Indians extended beyond the borders of the state. For an introduction to the collection, see John K. Weatherford, "Warren King Moorehead and His Papers," *Ohio Hist. Quart.*, 65 (1956), 179-190.

At the Wisconsin State Historical Society, Madison, is the manuscript collection assembled by one of the earliest and most voracious of American collectors, Lyman C. Draper, whose specialty was the frontier history of the trans-Allegheny region. The collection consists of 486 volumes of originals and copies and includes important runs of papers by and about Boone, Brant, Brodhead, George Rogers Clark, William Clark, Croghan, Harmar, Harrison, Kenton, Preston, Shepherd, and Tecumseh. See Reuben G. Thwaites, *Descriptive List* . . . (Madison, 1906), and Alice E. Smith, *Guide to the Manuscripts* . . . (Madison, 1944). The Draper Collection has been published on microfilm and is available for purchase in this form in parts or complete. William B.

Hesseltine has written a biography of Draper entitled *Pioneer's Mission: The Story of Lyman Copeland Draper* (Madison, 1954).

The collections of the Minnesota Historical Society have been described in its *Guide to the Personal Papers in the Manuscript Collections of the Minnesota Historical Society,* Vol. I (St. Paul, 1935) comp. Grace L. Nute and Gertrude W. Ackermann, and Vol. II (St. Paul, 1955) comp. Lucille N. Kane and K. A. Johnson.

The Missouri Historical Society, St. Louis, has more than 1500 manuscripts, covering the period 1766-1839, of William Clark, superintendent of Indian affairs at St. Louis and governor of Missouri Territory. Other Clark papers are in the Kansas Historical Society, Topeka.

The recently established Thomas Gilcrease Institute of American History and Art at Tulsa, Oklahoma, promises to become a major center for Indian studies because of its extensive holding in MSS, printed works, and iconographic material. A brief description is in *History News,* March, 1956, p. 37.

Far West

The Henry E. Huntington Library, San Marino, California, has important collections of colonial documents, many of which deal with Indian affairs. Especially noteworthy are the papers of William Blathwayt (1649-1717), General James Abercromby (1706-1781), and John Campbell, fourth Earl of Loudoun (1705-1782); the Robert Alonzo Brock collection of documents relating to Virginia and the South; and the Walter Channing Wyman Collection of manuscript Indian treaties and other documents relating to Indian affairs (many of which antedate 1800). The Library has, in addition, nearly all the printed Indian treaties of the colonial period. There is no complete printed catalogue of this material, but information can be obtained from the *Huntington Library Bulletin,* No. 1 (Cambridge, Mass., 1931), 33-106, and from later issues of the *Bulletin* and the *Bulletin's* successor, the *Huntington Library Quarterly.*

Canada

The principal Canadian repository of manuscript sources useful for the student of American Indian-white relations is the Public Archives of Canada, Ottawa. The Manuscript Division is engaged on a long range program, and is succeeding admirably, to secure either as originals, letter book copies, transcript copies by highly trained archival secretaries, or some form of photoduplication, all of the pertinent manuscripts dealing with the administration of Canada starting from the earliest days of New France. This includes the activities of full time agents who are continuously combing European archives and repositories to add to the Public Archives' collections from these sources. In addition to public papers the Archives also acts as a repository for many special and private collections. The Indian material contained in many of these various holdings is considerable.

The staff of the Public Archives is making guides and calendars of many of the collections and series, a process which has been going on for over sixty years. Since 1890 these have appeared in the annual reports, and constitute an invaluable tool for the scholar. Presently the Manuscript Division is preparing and printing in pamphlet form two series of preliminary inventories: those of record groups which are official records; and those of manuscript groups concerning private papers, and transcripts or photographic copies of papers in other depositories. Already published, for example, are the inventories of *Record Group 10: Indian Affairs* (Ottawa, 1951), and *Manuscript Group 19: Fur Trade and Indians, 1763-1867* (Ottawa, 1954). In addition to published calendars and inventories, other unpublished guides have been prepared for several of the important series of manuscripts. There is an excellent "Guide to Calendars of Series and Collections in the Public Archives," and an outline of "Series and Collections Having Registers or Descriptive Lists," in William Kaye Lamb, *Report of the Public Archives for the Year 1949* (Ottawa, 1950), pp. 451-462.

There are numerous other major Canadian repositories of manuscript sources. The Provincial Archives of Ontario, Toronto, contains, for example, a great bulk of John Graves Simcoe papers. The Archives du Séminaire de Québec, Université Laval, Québec, has among its rich holdings the Contrecoeur papers, some of which have been published under the editorship of Fernand Grenier (see § VI). The Archives of the Oblate Fathers, Scolasticat St. Joseph, Ottawa, contains valuable linguistic materials concerning the Indians of Eastern Canada. The Archives of the National Museum of Canada, Ottawa, possesses unpublished twentieth-century studies and materials dealing with Iroquois, Abitibi, Beothuc, Malecite, Micmac, Ojibwa, Huron, and Wyandot Indians. The Baby papers of the important early French Indian traders are in the library of the Université de Montréal, but, unfortunately, they are not readily accessible. The researcher should not overlook the holdings of various other universities such as Ottawa University, the provincial archives such as that of Quebec, municipal libraries such as that at Montreal, and the libraries of religious orders such as the Jesuit Seminary in Montreal.

In addition to the annual *Reports* and numerous inventories of the Public Archives, guides to the materials available in Canada include David W. Parker, *Guide to the Materials for United States History in Canadian Archives* (Wash.: Carnegie Institution, 1913); and David W. Parker, *A Guide to the Documents in the Manuscript Room at the Public Archives of Canada,* Publications of the Archives of Canada, No. 10 (Ottawa, 1914).

Microfilm

An important class of primary materials microfilmed by the State Records Microfilm Project, inaugurated jointly by the Library of Congress and the University of North Carolina, is the "Records of American-Indian Nations," Class M of the project. Part 1 of this class contains the records of official relations between the colonial and early state governments and the Indian tribes. There are sixteen reels of this material, filmed in historical societies and state archives, principally in Massachusetts, Connecticut, Rhode Island, New York, Pennsylvania, and South Carolina. A description of these records is contained in *A Guide to the Microfilm Collection of Early State Records: Supplement,* edited by William Sumner Jenkins (Wash., 1951), and in Mr. Jenkins' "Records of the States: Supplementary Microfilms," Lib. Cong., *Quarterly Journal of Current Acquisitions,* 13 (1955-1956), 12-16.

The student will frequently have to turn to foreign archives for material bearing on his studies of the American Indian. The immense British Manuscript Project of the American Council of Learned Societies (2,652 reels) is now catalogued in *A Checklist of the Microfilms Prepared in England and Wales for the American Council of Learned Societies, 1941-1945,* compiled by Lester K. Born (Wash., 1955). Documents from the Colonial Office papers of the Public Record Office, London, are especially noteworthy in this collection. It should be remembered, however, that American materials comprise only a small part of the collections microfilmed. A microfilm project to locate, list, and microfilm Virginia's colonial records in Great Britain and France is being carried out by a Subcommittee on Colonial Records set up under the joint federal-state commission organizing Virginia's 350th Anniversary Celebration for 1957. The project, under the direction of William J. Van Schreeven of the Virginia State Library, Richmond, will probably not complete its work until several years after the close of the Jamestown Festival. Once the project is concluded, it is expected that the microfilm will become available for purchase.

Almost as significant for the researcher as the projects for microfilming manuscript materials are the numerous plans for republishing early and rare books by microphotography. The most ambitious project underway is the publication on Microprint cards of every extant book, pamphlet, and broadside printed in the United States from 1639 through 1800, an enterprise sponsored by the American Antiquarian Society of Worcester, Massachusetts. For a description of the various undertakings, see Albert D. Van Nostrand, "The Micro-publication of Reprints," *American Studies,* Vol. 2, No. 2 (November, 1956), 1-3. The increasing availability of cheap microfilm copies of foreign and domestic materials gives scholars at small institutions the same opportunity to do advanced research previously reserved to traveling scholars or scholars resident at larger universities.

PART VI

DOCUMENTARY PUBLICATIONS

Alvord, Clarence W., ed., *The Cahokia Records, 1778-1790,* Ill. State Hist. Lib., *Colls.,* 2 (1907). 663 p., illus., bibliog.

Alvord, Clarence W., ed., *Kaskaskia Records, 1778-1790,* Ill. State Hist. Lib., *Colls.,* 5 (1909). 681 p., illus.

American State Papers: Documents, Legislative and Executive, of the Congress of the United States . . ., ed. Walter Lowrie and others (Wash., 1832-1834). 2 vols. Half-title: "Class II. Indian Affairs."

The basic collection of documents on the relations of the federal government with the Indians, 1789-1827. Other "classes" in this great series are also pertinent to Indian policy, wars, etc., for example, Class I. Foreign Relations (1833-1859), 6 vols; Class V. Military Affairs (1832-1861), 7 vols.; and Class VIII. Public Lands (1832-1861), 8 vols.

[Benton, Thomas Hart, ed.] *Abridgment of the Debates of Congress, from 1789 to 1856* [actually 1850] (N. Y., 1857-1861). 16 vols.

"Benton's Abridgment" is the most convenient collection of congressional debates. Indexes in each volume include both subjects and speakers; see under "Indian affairs," "Indian Lands," and similar entries. Compiled from the old *Annals, Register,* and *Globe,* the *Abridgment* is a selection but contains a mass of material very hard to locate in any other form, and it serves as a guide to the more extended official printings of the debates in Congress.

Blair, Emma H., *The Indian Tribes of the Upper Mississippi Valley and Region of the Great Lakes . . .* (Cleveland, 1911). 2 vols., map, bibliog.

A collection of descriptive accounts by French and American observers, ca. 1680-1827.

Bouquet, Henry, *Papers,* ed. S. K. Stevens and others. *Volume II: The Forbes Expedition* (Harrisburg, 1951). 704 p., illus., facsims.

Vol. II is the only volume so far published in letterpress though an extensive series of *The Papers of Col. Henry Bouquet* was issued in mimeographed form (Harrisburg, 1940-1943), 19 vols.

Boyd, Julian P., and Carl Van Doren, eds., *Indian Treaties Printed by Benjamin Franklin, 1736-1762* (Phila., 1938). 340 p., map.

Facsimiles of 13 Indian treaties printed by Franklin, with an introduction on the treaties as literature by Carl Van Doren, and an essay on "Indian Affairs in Pennsylvania, 1736-1762," by Julian P. Boyd; also bibliographical notes, extracts from journals of Pennsylvania commissioners at the conferences, "Glossary of Trade Terms," etc.

Burnett, Edmund C., ed., *Letters of Members of the Continental Congress* [1774-1789] (Wash., 1921-1936). 8 vols.

Carter, Clarence E., ed., *The Territorial Papers of the United States* (Wash., 1934-).

The 21 volumes so far published relate mainly to the area between the Alleghanies and the Mississippi. The criteria by which documents have been selected for publication have resulted in less emphasis on Indian affairs than on other aspects of territorial history. However, much of the material omitted from the printed volumes is available on microfilm. For a discussion by the editor of the problems that had to be faced in the publication of this series, see Clarence E. Carter, "The Territorial Papers of the United States: A Review and a Commentary," *Miss. Valley Hist. Rev.*, 42 (1955), 510-524.

Doublet de Boisthibault, François Jules, ed., *Les voeux des Hurons et des Abnaquis à Notre-Dame de Chartres publiés pour la première fois d'après les manuscrits des archives d'Eure-et-Loir, avec les lettres des missionnaires catholiques au Canada* (Chartres, 1857). 82 p., illus.

Grenier, Fernand, ed., *Papiers Contrecoeur et autres documents concernant le conflit anglo-français sur l'Ohio de 1745 à 1756* (Quebec, 1952). 485 p., maps, illus., facsims., bibliog.

The first of a projected series of publications of important documents from the Archives du Séminaire de Québec, Université Laval.

Griswold, Bert J., ed., *Fort Wayne, Gateway of the West, 1802-1813: Garrison Orderly Books; Indian Agency Account Book*, Ind. Hist. Bur., *Colls.*, 25 (1927). 690 p., maps., illus.

Harrison, William Henry, *Messages and Letters* [as Governor of Indiana Territory, 1800-1816], ed. Logan Esarey, Ind. Hist. Bur., *Colls.,* 7, 9 (1922). 744, 772 p.

Hough, Franklin Benjamin, comp., *Papers* [1641-1692] *Relating to the Island of Nantucket, with Documents Relating to the Original Settlement of that Island, Martha's Vineyard, and Other Islands Adjacent, Known as Duke's County, while under the Colony of New York* (Albany, 1856). 162 p., map, facsims.

Illinois State Historical Library. Springfield. *Collections,* 1903-   ·

Documents dealing with Illinois in the 17th and 18th centuries have been published in volumes of the "British Series," "French Series," "Virginia Series," "Law Series," and "Bibliographical Series" edited by such men as Clarence W. Alvord, James A. James, Clarence E. Carter, Theodore C. Pease, and Solon J. Buck. Other publications of the Library have been indexed in an *Index to the Transactions of the Illinois State Historical Society and Other Publications of the Illinois State Historical Library,* comp. James N. Adams (Springfield, 1953), 2 vols.

Indiana Historical Bureau. Indianapolis. Archaeological Reports of Indiana counties, 1924-   ·

Indiana Historical Society. Indianapolis. *Prehistory Research Series,* 1937-   ·

Irving, John Treat, Jr., *Indian Sketches Taken during an Expedition to the Pawnee Tribes* [1833], ed. John Francis McDermott (Norman, Okla., 1955). 275 p., map, illus., bibliog.

James, James A., ed., *George Rogers Clark Papers, 1771-1781,* Ill. State Hist. Lib., *Colls.,* 8 (1912). 715 p., illus.

Vol. III of "Virginia Series."

James, James A., ed., *George Rogers Clark Papers, 1781-1784,* Ill. State Hist. Lib., *Colls.,* 19 (1926). 572 p.

Vol. IV of "Virginia Series."

Jameson, J. Franklin, ed., *Original Narratives of Early American History* (N. Y., 1906-1917). 19 vols., maps, facsims.

One of these admirably edited collections of sources for 17th- and 18th-century history is devoted wholly to Indian relations (*Narratives of the Indian Wars, 1675-1699,* ed. Charles H. Lincoln), and nearly all the rest contain substantial descriptive and narrative material on the natives encountered.

Johnson, Sir William, *Papers,* ed. James Sullivan and others (Albany, 1921-   ). 11 vols. to date, maps, illus., facsims.

A scholarly edition issued under the supervision of the New York State Historian, the collection is based on the Johnson MSS in the N. Y. State Lib., but an ever-widening search for additional letters and documents by, to, and concerning Johnson was made in the course of publication, with the result that Vol. 9 begins a new chronological sequence. To be completed by Milton W. Hamilton in a 12th volume and general index. See also O'Callaghan, *Documentary History of the State of New York,* below.

Kellogg, Louise Phelps, ed., *Frontier Advance on the Upper Ohio, 1778-1779,* Wis. Hist. Soc., *Colls.,* 23 (1916). 509 p., map, illus., facsim.

Kellogg, Louise Phelps, ed., *Frontier Retreat on the Upper Ohio, 1779-1781,* Wis. Hist. Soc., *Colls.,* 24 (1917). 549 p., maps, illus., facsim.

Kinnaird, Lawrence, ed., *Spain in the Mississippi Valley, 1765-1794: Translations of Materials from the Spanish Archives in the Bancroft Library,* Amer. Hist. Assoc., *Ann. Report,* 1945, Vols. II-IV (Wash., 1946-1949).

Kingsbury, Susan M., ed., *The Records of the Virginia Company of London* (Wash., 1906-1935). 4 vols.

Laws of the Colonial and State Governments, Relating to Indians and Indian Affairs, from 1633 to 1831, Inclusive: With an Appendix Containing the Proceedings of the Congress of the Confederation and the Laws of Congress, from 1800 to 1830, on the Same Subject (Wash., 1832). 250, 72 p.

Colonial and state laws arranged geographically by colonies and states. Not a government publication.

Leder, Lawrence H., ed., *The Livingston Indian Records, 1666-1723* (Gettysburg, Pa., 1956). 240 p.

Papers of Robert Livingston, Secretary for Indian Affairs of the colony of New York. With "The Iroquois: A Brief Outline of Their History" by Paul A. W. Wallace, pp. 15-28; and a pictographic history of the founding of the Five Nations by Ray Fadden (Aren Akweks), pp. 28-199 (as footnotes).

Margry, Pierre, ed., *Découvertes et établissements des français dans l'ouest et dans le sud de l'Amérique Septentrionale (1614-1754): Mémoires et documents originaux* . . . (Paris, 1876-1886). 6 vols., illus.

French narratives of discovery and exploration in North America, 1614-1754.

Maryland. *Archives of Maryland*. 1883-   .

Since publication of the *Proceedings and Acts of the General Assembly, 1637/8-1664,* ed. William Hand Browne, in 1883, the Maryland Historical Society has managed to bring out nearly one volume of Maryland colonial records per year.

Massachusetts Historical Society. Boston. *Collections,* 1792-   .

The historical societies and state archival agencies of New England and other sections of the country have printed great amounts of documentary material dealing with the colonial history of their areas. The *Collections* of the Mass. Hist. Soc. is a particularly distinguished source. The student should check the indexes, guides, and tables of contents of all the collections published by these bodies for references to Indian-white relations.

Michigan Historical Commission (Pioneer Society of the State of Michigan, 1874-1886; Pioneer and Historical Society of the State of Michigan, 1887-1912). Lansing. *Historical Collections,* 1874-1929.

Mulkearn, Lois, ed., *George Mercer Papers Relating to the Ohio Company of Virginia* (Pittsburgh, 1954). 731 p., maps, illus., bibliog.

Among other documents bearing on Indian affairs, this collection contains Christopher Gist's journals of exploration in the upper Ohio Valley, 1750-1752. The notes contain encyclopedic data on Indian tribes, villages, and leaders.

Nasatir, Abraham P., ed., *Before Lewis and Clark: Documents Illustrating the History of the Missouri, 1785-1804* (St. Louis, 1952). 2 vols., maps.

New York. *Documents Relative to the Colonial History of the State of New York; procured in Holland, England and France,* ed. E. B. O'Callaghan, John Romeyn Brodhead, and B. Fernow (Albany, 1853-1887). 15 vols.

Vols. XII-XV consist of documents taken principally from American sources.

New York State. Division of Archives and History. *The Sullivan-Clinton Campaign in 1779: Chronology and Selected Documents* (Albany, 1929). 216 p., maps, illus., facsims., bibliog.

See the following entry (*Journals* of the Sullivan Campaign);

also Alexander C. Flick, "New Sources on the Sullivan-Clinton Campaign in 1779," N. Y. State Hist. Assoc., *Quart. Jour.,* 10 (1929), 185-224, 265-317.

New York State. Secretary of State. *Journals of the Military Expedition of Major General John Sullivan against the Six Nations of Indians in 1779* (Auburn, 1887). 580 p., maps, illus.

Prints 26 officers' journals, some of them very extensive, together with Sullivan's official report and other contemporary documents and historical addresses relating to the single major operation against the Indians during the Revolution. Of major importance for understanding the attitude of Americans toward the Indians in the late 18th century.

O'Callaghan, E. B., ed., *The Documentary History of the State of New York* . . . (Albany, 1849-1851). 4 vols., maps, illus.

Contains a mass of indiscriminately arranged source material, including Indian treaties, drawn from the State archives and foreign repositories and extending from the early 17th to the early 19th century. Volumes II and IV contain over 800 pages of Sir William Johnson papers not reprinted in the current edn. of the *Sir William Johnson Papers;* those in Vol. IV deal especially with religious and educational work among the Six Nations.

Pargellis, Stanley M., ed., *Military Affairs in North America, 1748-1765: Selected Documents from the Cumberland Papers in Windsor Castle* (N. Y., 1936). 514 p., maps.

Peckham, Howard H., ed., *George Croghan's Journal of his Trip to Detroit in 1767, with his Correspondence relating thereto* (Ann Arbor, 1939). 61 p.

Pennsylvania. *Colonial Records.* 1838-1853. Succeeded by *Pennsylvania Archives.* 1852-   .

Henry Howard Eddy has compiled a *Guide to the Published Archives of Pennsylvania covering the 138 volumes of Colonial Records and Pennsylvania Archives, Series I-IX* (Harrisburg, 1949).

Pike, Zebulon M., *An Account of Expeditions to the Sources of the Mississippi, and through the Western Parts of Louisiana, to the Sources of the Arkansaw, Kans, La Platte, and Pierre Jaun Rivers;*

Performed by order of the Government of the United States during the years 1805, 1806, and 1807 (Phila., 1810). 277, 65, 53, 87 p., maps, illus.

Quinn, David Beers, ed., *The Roanoke Voyages, 1584-1590: Documents to Illustrate the English Voyages to North America Under the Patent Granted to Sir Walter Raleigh in 1584* (London, 1955). 2 vols., maps, illus., bibliog.

A publication of the Hakluyt Society (2d ser., No. CIV), these volumes contain a great mass of information, in the form of both documents and historical and scientific discussion, on the Carolina Algonquian Indians encountered by the English adventurers who planted the "lost colony" on Roanoke Island. Nearly six columns of the subject index are devoted to topics relating to Indians. The collection includes the full text of Thomas Hariot's *Briefe and True Report of the New Found Land of Virginia* (London, 1588), "the most delectable of Americana" (Quinn, I, 37) and the first considerable English account of North American ethnology.

Richardson, James H., ed., *A Compilation of the Messages and Papers of the Presidents* (Wash., 1896-1899). 10 vols.

Various later edns. Vols. I-III, 1789-1841, naturally contain many pronouncements concerning Indian policy.

Robertson, Nellie A., and Dorothy Riker, eds., *The John Tipton Papers* [1809-1839], comp. by Glen A. Blackburn, Ind. Hist. Bur., *Colls.*, 24-26 (1942).

Tipton, a leading figure in Indiana in the period when Indian occupancy was replaced by white, served variously as Indian fighter, surveyor, land speculator, Indian agent, and United States Senator. The "Introduction" to the Papers, written by Paul Wallace Gates, gives an excellent biographical sketch of Tipton.

Rowland, Dunbar, and Albert G. Sanders, eds., *Mississippi Provincial Archives: French Dominion* [1701-1740] (Jackson, 1927-1932). 3 vols.

Dunbar Rowland has also edited *Mississippi Provincial Archives: English Dominion, 1763-1766* (Nashville, 1911), and *Mississippi Territorial Archives, 1798-1803* (Nashville, 1905).

Scull, Gideon D., ed., *Voyages of Peter* [Pierre] *Esprit Radisson, Being an Account of His Travels and Experiences Among the*

North American Indians, from 1652 to 1684 (Boston, 1885). 385 p. Prince Society, *Pubns.*, Vol. XVI. Repr. N. Y., 1943.

Smith, William H., ed., *The St. Clair Papers: The Life and Public Services of Arthur St. Clair, . . . with His Correspondence and Other Papers* (Cincinnati, 1882). 2 vols., map, illus.

South Carolina. *The Colonial Records of South Carolina* [Series 2: The Indian Books], *Journals of the Commissioners of the Indian Trade, September 20, 1710—August 29, 1718,* ed. W. L. McDowell (Columbia, 1955). 368 p., illus.

The South Carolina Archives Department plans to publish its whole collection of Indian Books as the Second Series of its *Colonial Records.* Three more volumes are projected.

Stevens, Sylvester K., and Donald H. Kent, eds., *Wilderness Chronicles of Northwestern Pennsylvania* (Harrisburg, 1941). 342 p., maps, illus., bibliog.

A selection of documents from French and English sources relating to imperial rivalry and Indian affairs in the Upper Ohio Valley, 1728-1764.

Thwaites, Reuben G., ed., *Early Western Travels, 1748-1846 . . .* (Cleveland, 1904-1907). 32 vols., illus., maps, facsims.

Includes reprints of the journals and travels of Weiser, Croghan, Post, John Long, Bradbury, Brackenridge, Estwick Evans, Nuttall, Prince Maximilian.

Thwaites, Reuben G., ed., *The Jesuit Relations and Allied Documents: Travels and Explorations of the Jesuit Missionaries in New France, 1610-1791. The Original French, Latin, and Italian Texts with English Translations and Notes* (Cleveland, 1896-1901). 73 vols., maps, illus., facsim.

A 2-volume selection from this collection was edited by Edna Kenton under the title *The Indians of North America* (N. Y., 1925); new edn., 1954.

Thwaites, Reuben G., ed., *Original Journals of the Lewis and Clark Expedition, 1804-1806 . . .* (N. Y., 1904-1905). 8 vols., of which the last is an atlas.

An excellent 1-volume abridgment was edited by Bernard DeVoto (Boston, 1953).

Thwaites, Reuben G., and Louise Phelps Kellogg, eds., *Documentary*

History of Dunmore's War, 1774 . . . (Madison, Wis., 1905). 472 p., maps, facsim.

Thwaites, Reuben G., and Louise Phelps Kellogg, eds., *Frontier Defense on the Upper Ohio, 1777-1778* . . . (Madison, Wis., 1912). 329 p., map, illus., facsims.

Thwaites, Reuben G., and Louise Phelps Kellogg, eds., *The Revolution on the Upper Ohio, 1775-1777* (Madison, Wis., 1908). 275 p., map, illus.

Treaties, Collections of. See in this section Boyd and Van Doren, *Indian Treaties,* and entries under U. S., Treaties; also De Puy, *Bibliography* (§ I), and Cohen, *Handbook* (§ VII, F).

U. S. Continental Congress. *Journals . . . , 1774-1789,* ed. Worthington C. Ford and others (Wash., 1904-1937). 34 vols., facsims.

U. S. Laws and Treaties. *Indian Affairs: Laws and Treaties,* ed. Charles J. Kappler, 58th Congress, 2d sess., Senate Doc. 319 (Wash., 1903). 2 vols.

Repr. 1904. I: Statutes, executive orders, proclamations, and statistics of tribes [from 1832]. II: Treaties [from 1778]. Later volumes print laws and treaties up to date (1941).

U. S. Treaties. *Indian Treaties between the United States and the Indian Tribes,* comp. under the supervision of the Commissioner of Indian Affairs (Wash., 1837).

"More comprehensive than any other edition covering the same period [1778-1837]. . . . The compiler's notes are accurate and labor-saving" (Abel, Amer. Hist. Assoc., *Ann. Report,* 1906, I, 425).

U. S. Treaties. *A Compilation of All the Treaties between the United States and the Indian Tribes, Now in Force as Laws. Prepared under the Provisions of the Act of Congress, Approved March 3, 1873* (Wash., 1873). 1075 p.

Treaties arranged alphabetically by tribes.

U. S. Treaties. *Indian Treaties, and Laws and Regulations Relating to Indian Affairs: To Which Is Added an Appendix, Containing the Proceedings of the Old Congress, and Other Important State Papers, in Relation to Indian Affairs* (Wash., 1825). 529 p. Reissued with same title page but with a "Supplement" of Treaties, etc., to end of 21st Congress (Wash. [1831?]); 661 p.

"Compiled and published under orders of the Department of

War." Samuel S. Hamilton, compiler. Valuable because it concentrates on the early period and provides documents and statistics on Indian tribes just at the time of the Removal controversy.

Williams, Samuel C., ed., *Early Travels in the Tennessee Country, 1540-1800* (Johnson City, Tenn., 1928). 540 p., maps, illus., facsims.

Selections from accounts by explorers and travelers from DeSoto (1540-1541) to the Moravian mission to the Cherokee Indians (1799).

PART VII

SPECIAL TOPICS

A. Portraiture

Bushnell, David I., Jr., "Drawings by A. De Batz in Louisiana, 1732-1735," Smithsonian *Misc. Colls.,* 80, No. 5 (Wash., 1927). 14 p., illus.

>Drawings of Mississippi Valley Indians (Fox, Illinois, Atakapa), showing dress, hair style, etc.

Catlin, George, *Letters and Notes on the Manners, Customs, and Condition of the North American Indians* (N. Y., 1841). 2 vols., maps, illus.

>1st edn. of a famous work reprinted frequently since. Written during eight years' travel, 1832-1839, among the Indian tribes of the West. Hundreds of illustrations, based on Catlin's paintings and sketches, accompany the text of most edns. Catlin's collection of paintings and sketches was presented to the Smithsonian Institution in 1879.

DeVoto, Bernard, "The First Illustrators of the West," App. 2 in *Across the Wide Missouri* (Boston, 1947), pp. 391-415.

>George Catlin, George Bodmer, Alfred Jacob Miller, with a brief review of earlier artists.

Ewers, John C., "An Anthropologist Looks at Early Pictures of North American Indians," N. Y. Hist. Soc., *Quart.,* 33 (1949), 222-234.

Fenton, William N., "The Hyde de Neuville Portraits of New York Savages in 1807-1808," N. Y. Hist. Soc., *Quart.,* 38 (1954), 118-137, 10 plates.

Hariot, Thomas, *Narrative of the First English Plantation of Virginia by Thomas Hariot; First printed at London in 1588; now reproduced after [Theodore] De Bry's illustrated edition printed at Frankfort in 1590 the illustrations having been designed in Virginia in 1588 by John White* (London, 1893). 112 p., illus.

>A biography of Hariot, one of the foremost scientists of his day, is being prepared by John W. Shirley of North Carolina State College.

Hunter, H. Chadwick, "The American Indian in Painting," *Art and Archaeology*, 8 (1919), 81-96.

LeMoyne, Jacques, *Narrative of LeMoyne, an Artist who Accompanied the French Expedition to Florida under Laudonnière, 1564. Translated from the Latin of De Bry* (Boston, 1875). 23, 15 p., map, illus.

Lorant, Stefan, ed., *The New World: the First Pictures of America, Made by John White and Jacques Le Moyne and Engraved by Theodore De Bry, with Contemporary Narratives of the Huguenot Settlement in Florida, 1562-1565, and the Virginia Colony, 1585-1590* (N. Y., 1946). 292 p., maps, illus., bibliog.

The reproductions of John White's watercolor drawings of Indians and Indian scenes at the "lost" English colony on Roanoke Island, North Carolina, are not reliable because not taken directly from the celebrated originals in the British Museum. An authoritative edition of the whole body of White's drawings, in colored collotype with full descriptive notes, is in preparation and will be jointly published by the British Museum and the University of North Carolina Press, probably in 1958.

McKenney, Thomas L., and James Hall, *History of the Indian Tribes of North America* (Phila., 1836-1844). 3 vols., illus.

A collection of portraits, accompanied by biographical sketches, based on the "Indian Gallery" of the U. S. War Department, a collection begun in 1821 by McKenney when he was a federal Indian official. For bibliographical data and notes on the artists, see F. W. Hodge's valuable Introd. to Edinburgh edn. (3 vols., 1933-1934).

Weitenkampf, Frank, "Early Pictures of North American Indians: A Question of Ethnology," N. Y. Public Lib., *Bull.*, 53 (1949), 591-614.

Weitenkampf, Frank, "How Indians Were Pictured in Earlier Days," N. Y. Hist. Soc., *Quart.*, 33 (1949), 213-221.

Winter, George, *The Journals and Indian Paintings of George Winter, 1837-1839* (Indianapolis: Indiana Hist. Soc., 1948). 208 p., illus.

Howard H. Peckham contributes an "Introduction," Wilbur D. Peat discusses "Winter the Artist," and Gayle Thornbrough provides a careful biographical study.

See also under § III, B: Bond, *Queen Anne's American Kings;* Gabriel,

Lure of the Frontier; under § III, A: Foster, *Jeffersonian America;* under § VII, F: Brinton, "Benjamin West's Painting . . . ."

B. Literature, Songs, and Art

Astrov, Margot, ed., *The Winged Serpent: An Anthology of American Indian Prose and Poetry* (N. Y., 1946). 366 p., bibliog.
　　Extends geographically from the Eskimos to Peru.

Austin, Mary, "Non-English Writings, II: Aboriginal," *Cambridge Hist. of Amer. Lit.,* IV (N. Y., 1921), 610-634, 826-827 (bibliog.).
　　Discussion, with excerpts, of Indian literature.

Brinton, Daniel G., *Aboriginal American Authors and Their Productions* (Phila., 1883). 63 p.

Brinton, Daniel G., *The Lenâpé and Their Legends, with the Complete Text and Symbols of the Walum Olum* . . . (Phila., 1885). 262 p.
　　No. V in Brinton's *Libr. of Aboriginal Amer. Lit.*

Canfield, William W., *The Legends of the Iroquois, Told by "The Cornplanter"* (N. Y., 1902). 219 p., illus.

Converse, Harriet Maxwell, *Myths and Legends of the New York State Iroquois,* N. Y. State Mus., *Bull.* 125 (Albany, 1908). 195 p., illus.

Cronyn, George W., ed., *The Path on the Rainbow: An Anthology of Songs and Chants from the Indians of North America* (new edn., N. Y., 1934). 360 p., illus.
　　1st edn. 1918.

Day, Arthur Grove, *The Sky Clears: Poetry of the American Indians* (N. Y., 1951). 204 p., bibliog., index.
　　An anthology of American Indian poetry in English translation based on a dissertation in English literature. Combines literary criticism with ethnographic sampling and presentation by culture areas. Selection shows range and diversity of humanistic content and expression.

Densmore, Frances, *The American Indians and Their Music* (N. Y., 1926). 143 p., illus., bibliog.

Douglas, Frederic H., and René d'Harnoncourt, *Indian Art of the United States* (N. Y., 1941). 219 p., illus., bibliog.
　　A look at Indian art is one of the best ways to understand why scientists are unhappy with the misleading word "primitive."

Fenton, William N., *The Iroquois Eagle Dance: An Offshoot of the Calumet Dance. With an Analysis of the Iroquois Eagle Dance and Songs by Gertrude Prokosch Kurath.* Bur. of Amer. Ethnol., *Bull.* 156 (Wash., 1953). 324 p., maps, 28 pls., 36 figs., bibliogs.

Commenced as a dissertation at Yale on a problem in field ethnology, this work combines protracted field work over two decades with comparative ethnography and historical documentation. Kurath, analyzing the music and treating it comparatively, devised new techniques for the study of music and the dance and reached the same historical conclusions independently, that the Eagle Dance derives from the Calumet Dance of the mid-Mississippi area.

Hale, Horatio, *The Iroquois Book of Rites* (Phila., 1883). 222 p.

No. II in Brinton's *Libr. of Amer. Aboriginal Lit.*

Hamilton, Charles E., ed., *Cry of the Thunderbird: The American Indian's Own Story* (N. Y., 1950). 283 p., illus., bibliog.

Hewitt, J. N. B., and Jeremiah Curtin, *Seneca Fiction, Legends, and Myths,* Bur. Amer. Ethnol., 32d *Ann. Report,* 1910-1911 (Wash., 1918), 37-814.

Jacobson, Oscar B., and Jeanne d'Ucel, *Les peintres indiens d'Amérique* (Nice, 1950). 2 vols. 77 col. plates.

Nettl, Bruno, *North American Indian Musical Styles,* American Folklore Society, *Memoirs,* 45 (Phila., 1954). 51 p.

Parker, Arthur C., *Seneca Myths and Folk Tales* (Buffalo, 1923). 465 p., bibliog.

Swanton, John R., ed., *Myths and Tales of the Southeastern Indians,* Bur. Amer. Ethnol., *Bull.* 88 (Wash., 1929). 275 p.

Thompson, Stith, ed., *Tales of the North American Indians* (Cambridge, Mass., 1929). 386 p., map, bibliog.

Vaillant, George C., *Indian Arts in North America* (N. Y., 1939). 63 p., 96 plates, bibliog.

Indian art, formerly ignored or misunderstood, has become more appreciated as its meaning has become more intelligible to outsiders.

Walam Olum or Red Score: The Migration Legend of the Lenni Lenape or Delaware Indians. A New Translation, Interpreted by Linguistic, Historical, Archaeological, Ethnological, and Physical Anthropological Studies [Contributors: C. F. Voegelin, J. E. Pierce,

Paul Weer, Eli Lilly, Erminie Voegelin, G. A. Black, G. K. Neu-
mann], (Indianapolis, 1954). 379 p.

Wallace, Paul A. W., *The White Roots of Peace* (Phila., 1946). 57 p.
A classic of Iroquois literature.

Wroth, Lawrence C., "The Indian Treaty as Literature," *Yale Rev.*,
17 (1928), 749-766. Repr. in Wroth's *A Colonial Bookshelf*.

On this subject see also Carl Van Doren's Introduction to the
Boyd-Van Doren edn. of *Indian Treaties Printed by Benjamin
Franklin* (§ VI above), and Drummond and Moody (§ VII, G
below).

See also under § I: Haywood, *Bibliography of North American Folklore and Folksongs*.

C. Biography and Autobiography

Black Hawk, *Ma-Ka-Tai-Me-She-Kia-Kiak: Black Hawk, An Autobiography*, ed. Donald Jackson (Urbana, Ill., 1955). 206 p., maps,
illus., bibliog.
Reprint of 1833 edn.

Caughey, John W., *McGillivray of the Creeks* (Norman, Okla., 1938).
385 p.

Chalmers, Harvey, *Joseph Brant: Mohawk* (East Lansing, Mich., 1955).
364 p., illus.
Of limited value to scholars because of the author's overstate-
ments, conjectures, and, at times, uncritical use of the sources.

Drake, Benjamin, *Life of Tecumseh, and of His Brother The Prophet;
with a Historical Sketch of the Shawanoe Indians* (Cincinnati,
1841). 235 p.

Drake, Samuel G., *Indian Biography Containing the Lives of More
than Two Hundred Indian Chiefs; also, Such Others of That Race
as Have Rendered Their Names Conspicuous in the History of
North America, from Its First Being Known to Europeans, to the
Present Period* ... (Boston, 1832). 350 p.
1st edn. of a work that went through many reprintings and revi-
sions with variant titles (*The Book of the Indians of North America,
Biography and History of the Indians of North America*).

Eaton, Rachel C., *John Ross and the Cherokee Indians* (Menasha, Wis.,
1914). 212 p., bibliog.

Foreman, Grant, *Sequoyah* (Norman, Okla., 1938). 90 p., illus.

"The definitive account of the great Cherokee genius" (Starkey, *Cherokee Nation*).

Gabriel, Ralph Henry, *Elias Boudinot, Cherokee, and His America* (Norman, Okla., 1941). 190 p., map., illus.

Educated in a mission school in Connecticut, Boudinot returned to his tribe in Georgia where he edited the *Cherokee Phoenix*.

Hubbard, John Niles, *An Account of Sa-Go-Ye-Wat-Ha, or Red Jacket and His People, 1750-1830* (Albany, 1886). 356 p.

Jones, Charles C., *Historical Sketch of Tomo-Chi-Chi, Mico of the Yamacraws* (Albany, 1868). 133 p.

Tomochichi, the Creek chief, was General Oglethorpe's valued Indian friend in the settlement of Georgia.

Kluckhohn, Clyde, "The Personal Document in Anthropological Science," in Louis Gottschalk and others, *The Use of Personal Documents in History, Anthropology, and Sociology*, Soc. Sci. Res. Council, *Bull.* 53 (N. Y., 1949), 79-173.

A guide for historians who would use Indian personal documents (diaries, letters, autobiographies). Full bibliography, pp. 164-173.

Lincecum, Gideon, "Life of Apushimataha," Mississippi Hist. Soc., *Pubns.*, 9 (Oxford, 1906), 415-485.

Written in 1861 by an acquaintance of Apushimataha, a Choctaw chief who died about 1824.

Meserve, Walter T., "English Works of Seventeenth-Century Indians," *American Quarterly*, 8 (1956), 264-276.

Peckham, Howard H., *Pontiac and the Indian Uprising* (Princeton, 1947). 346 p., bibliog.

Radin, Paul, ed. and trans., *Crashing Thunder: The Autobiography of an American Indian* (N. Y., 1926). 203 p.

The editor hopes that the autobiography of this twentieth-century Winnebago Indian "will play its role in dissipating once and for all the erroneous notion that still persists—that primitive peoples are incapable of an objective and analytical presentation of facts, that they can draw no clear line between truth and illusion, between hallucination and phantasy-dreaming on the one hand, and the objective world on the other."

Sipe, Chester Hale, *The Indian Chiefs of Pennsylvania* . . . (Butler, Penna., 1927). 569 p.
> Undocumented.

Stone, William L., *The Life and Times of Red Jacket, or Sa-Go-Ye-Wat-Ha* (N. Y., 1841). 484 p., illus.

Stone, William L., *Life of Joseph Brant—Thayendanegea: Including the Border Wars of the American Revolution, and Sketches of the Indian Campaigns of Generals Harmar, St. Clair, and Wayne* (N. Y., 1838). 2 vols., map., illus.
> Repr. 1865. A comprehensive work based on both sources and the memory of participants in the contests with the Indians, but rambling in its organization and highly apologetic in behalf of Brant.

Tucker, Glenn, *Tecumseh: Vision of Glory* (Indianapolis, 1956). 399 p., illus.

Wallace, Anthony F. C., *King of the Delawares: Teedyuscung, 1700-1763* (Phila., 1949). 305 p., bibliog.

Young, Calvin M., *Little Turtle (Me-she-kin-no-quah)* [d. 1812] *the Great Chief of the Miami Indian Nation* (Indianapolis, 1917). 249 p., illus., bibliog.

D. Captivities

Baker, C. Alice, *True Stories of New England Captives Carried to Canada during the Old French and Indian Wars* (Cambridge, 1897). 407 p., illus.

Barbeau, Marius, "Indian Captivities," Amer. Philos. Soc., *Procs.,* 94 (1950), 522-548.

Coleman, Emma Lewis, *New England Captives Carried to Canada between 1677 and 1760 during the French and Indian Wars* (Portland, Me., 1925). 2 vols., illus.
> A documentary account of Indian-white relations in New England during the century of Anglo-French rivalry for North America. A most important source collection, with admirable commentary.

Dickinson, Jonathan, *Jonathan Dickinson's Journal, or God's Protecting Providence. Being the Narrative of a Journey from Port Royal in Jamaica to Philadelphia between August 23, 1696 and April 1,*

1697, ed. Evangeline Andrews and Charles McLean Andrews (New Haven, 1945). 252 p., maps, illus.

Originally published Phila., 1699, and frequently reprinted; see Vail 281 and numerous other entries. Vail calls the Andrews edn. "The most scholarly edition of any story of Indian captivity."

Drake, Samuel G., ed., *Tragedies of the Wilderness; or, True and Authentic Narratives of Captives, Who Have Been Carried Away by the Indians from the Various Frontier Settlements of the United States, from the Earliest to the Present Time* (Boston, 1841). 360 p., illus.

Reprints about 25 captivity narratives from the 16th to the 19th century.

Pearce, Roy H., "The Significances of the Captivity Narrative," *Amer. Lit.,* 19 (1947), 1-20.

An attempt to show how the captivity varies in significance with the interests (political, religious, journalistic, etc.) of the narrator.

Peckham, Howard H., *Captured by Indians: True Tales of Pioneer Survivors* (New Brunswick, 1954). 238 p., illus.

A modern retelling, by a leading authority on the history of Indian-white relations, of 14 captivities, 1676-1864.

Rowlandson, Mary, *The Narrative of the Captivity and Restoration of Mrs. Mary Rowlandson* (Boston, 1930). 86 p., map, illus.

This is the most readily available separate printing of the first New England captivity narrative; original edition, Cambridge, Mass., 1682. See Vail 211-214 and later entries for bibliographical and historical details. The Rowlandson *Narrative* may also be found in C. H. Lincoln's *Narratives of the Indian Wars (Original Narratives of Early Amer. Hist.),* pp. 107-167.

Seaver, James E., *A Narrative of the Life of Mary Jemison, the White Woman of the Genesee,* ed. Charles D. Vail (22d edn., N. Y., 1925). 459 p., maps, illus., bibliog.

The first edition of this celebrated captivity narrative was published at Canandaigua, N. Y., 1824. Mary Jemison was captured in Pennsylvania in 1755 and spent the rest of her life among the Senecas. The narrative was "carefully taken from her own words" by Seaver. The present edition contains extensive commentary and notes.

Smith, Dwight L., "Shawnee Captivity Ethnography," *Ethnohistory,*
2 (1955), 29-41, bibliog.
Smith, James, *An Account of the Remarkable Occurrences in the Life
and Travels of Col. James Smith, . . . during His Captivity with
the Indians in the Years 1755, '56, '57, '58, & '59 . . .* (Lexington,
Ky., 1799). 88 p.
   One of the most important captivity narratives because of its historical and ethnological information. Frequently reprinted; there
was a Cincinnati edition, 1907, and a reprint will be found in *Magazine of History,* Extra No. 7 (1914). See W. R. Jillson, *A Bibliography of the Life and Writings of Col. James Smith* (Frankfort, Ky.,
1947).
Vail, Robert W. G., "The Indian Captives Relate Their Adventures,"
in his *The Voice of the Old Frontier* (Phila., 1949), 23-61.
See also under § I: Newberry Library, *Narratives of Captivity.*

E. Missions and Education

Alden, Timothy, *An Account of Sundry Missions Performed among
the Senecas and Munsees . . .* (N. Y., 1827). 180 p.
Beatty, Charles, *The Journal of a Two-Months Tour; with a View of
Promoting Religion among the Frontier Inhabitants of Pennsyl-
vania, and of Introducing Christianity among the Indians to the
Westward of the Alegh-geny Mountains. To Which Are Added,
Remarks on the Language and Customs of Some Particular Tribes
among the Indians, with a Brief Account of the Various Attempts
That Have Been Made to Civilize and Convert Them, from the
First Settlement of New England to This Day* (London, 1768),
110 p.
   An important journal that deserves a modern edition.
Blodgett, Harold, *Samson Occom* (Hanover, N. H., 1935). 230 p.,
bibliog.
DeSchweinitz, Edmund, *The Life and Times of David Zeisberger, the
Western Pioneer and Apostle of the Indians* (Phila., 1870). 747 p.
Eames, Wilberforce, ed., *John Eliot and the Indians, 1652-1657. Being
Letters Addressed to Rev. Jonathan Hanmer of Barnstaple, Eng-
land . . .* (N. Y., 1915). 31 p., facsims.

Edwards, Jonathan, *Memoirs of the Rev. David Brainerd; Missionary to the Indians on the Borders of New-York, New-Jersey, and Pennsylvania: Chiefly Taken from His Own Diary,* ed. Sereno Edwards Dwight (New Haven, 1822). 507 p.

   An enlarged edn. of Jonathan Edwards' *Account of the Life of the Late Rev. David Brainerd* (Boston, 1749).

[Eliot, John, The "Eliot Indian Tracts"]

   For the 11 so-called Eliot Indian Tracts issued in London in the interest of the Corporation for the Propagation of the Gospel among the Indians of New England, 1643-1671, see Vail 98, 108, 111, 114, 127, 131, 134, 142, 145, 158; also George Parker Winship, "The Eliot Indian Tracts," in *Bibliographical Essays, a Tribute to Wilberforce Eames* (N. Y., 1924), pp. 179-192. By various authors, not all certainly identified, these tracts narrate the missionary labors of John Eliot and Thomas Mayhew and contain important information on the Indians of eastern Massachusetts. Seven of the 11 tracts are reprinted in Mass. Hist. Soc., *Colls.,* 3d ser., 4 (1834). All are in the William L. Clements Library, Ann Arbor.

[Eliot's Indian Bible and Other Works on the Indian Language]

   See Wilberforce Eames, *Bibliographic Notes on Eliot's Indian Bible and on His Other Translations and Works in the Indian Language of Massachusetts* (Wash., 1890). 58 p., 21 facsims.

   Incorporated in Pilling's *Bibliography of the Algonquian Languages* (1891), 127-184.

Elsbree, Oliver W., *The Rise of the Missionary Spirit in America, 1790-1815* (Williamsport, Penna., 1928). 187 p., bibliog.

Finley, James B., *History of the Wyandott Mission at Upper Sandusky, Ohio* (Cincinnati, 1840). 432 p.

   Finley was a Methodist missionary among the Wyandotts.

Francis, Convers, *Life of John Eliot, the Apostle to the Indians* (Jared Sparks, ed., *The Library of American Biography,* V, Boston, 1836). 357 p.

[Friends, Society of], *Some Account of the Conduct of the Religious Society of Friends towards the Indian Tribes in the Settlement of the Colonies of East and West Jersey and Pennsylvania . . .* (London, 1844). 247 p., maps.

Gipson, Lawrence H., ed., *The Moravian Indian Mission on White*

River [Indiana Territory]: Diaries and Letters, May 5, 1799 to November 12, 1806, Ind. Hist. Bur., *Colls.*, 23 (1938). 674 p., illus.

Gray, Elma E., and Leslie Robb, *Wilderness Christians: The Moravian Mission to the Delaware Indians* (Ithaca, N. Y., 1956). 354 p., illus.

Hare, Lloyd C. M., *Thomas Mayhew, Patriarch to the Indians (1593-1682)* (N. Y., 1932). 231 p., maps, illus.

Hawkins, Ernest, *Historical Notices of the Missions of the Church of England in the North American Colonies Previous to the Independence of the United States* (London, 1845). 447 p.

Heckewelder, John, *A Narrative of the Mission of the United Brethren among the Delaware and Mohegan Indians, from Its Commencement, in the Year 1740, to the Close of the Year 1808* (Phila., 1820). 429 p., illus.

   An edition was published at Cleveland, 1907, ed. W. E. Connelly.

Jackson, Halliday, *Civilization of the Indian Natives; or, A Brief View of the Friendly Conduct of William Penn towards Them . . . ; the Subsequent Care of the Society of Friends . . . ; and a Concise Narrative of the Proceedings of the Yearly Meeting of Friends of Pennsylvania, New Jersey, . . . since . . . 1795, in Promoting Their Improvement and Gradual Civilization* (Philadelphia, 1830). 120 p.

   Some copies contain another item of outstanding excellence: "A Sketch of the Manners, Customs, Religion and Government of the Seneca Indians in 1800," [Philadelphia, 1830], 34 p.

   The author was one of three Quaker youths who worked among the Senecas at Allegheny River after 1798, witnessing the Seneca prophet's visions and the first introduction of farming among the Seneca men.

Kelsey, Rayner W., *Friends and the Indians, 1655-1917* (Phila., 1917). 291 p., illus., bibliog.

   A Quaker publication. The best introduction to the history of the Quaker missions to the Indians.

Kennedy, John H., *Jesuit and Savage in New France* (New Haven, 1950). 206 p., map, bibliog.

Loskiel, George Henry, *History of the Mission of the United Brethren among the Indians in North America. In Three Parts*, trans. Christian I. LaTrobe (London, 1794). 159, 234, 233 p.

Lothrop, Samuel K., "Life of Samuel Kirkland, Missionary to the Indians," in Jared Sparks, ed., *The Library of American Biography*, 2d ser., XV (Boston, 1848), 137-368.

Love, William DeLoss, *Samson Occom, and the Christian Indians of New England* (Boston, 1899). 379 p., map, illus.

Lydekker, John Wolfe, *The Faithful Mohawks* (Cambridge, England, 1938). 206 p., map, illus., bibliog.

Based largely on records of the Society for the Propagation of the Gospel, London.

McCallum, James Dow, *Eleazar Wheelock, Founder of Dartmouth College* (Hanover, N. H., 1939). 236 p.

Based on Wheelock's papers at Dartmouth.

McCallum, James Dow, ed., *The Letters of Eleazar Wheelock's Indians* (Hanover, N. H., 1932). 327 p., illus.

From originals in Dartmouth Coll. MSS.

McCoy, Isaac, *History of Baptist Indian Missions, Embracing Remarks on the Former and Present Condition of the Aboriginal Tribes . . .* (Wash. and N. Y., 1840). 611 p.

McCoy supervised the removal of some of the northern tribes to their Kansas reservations. His MS correspondence and journals are in the Kansas Hist. Soc.

Moore, Martin, *Memoirs of the Life and Character of Rev. John Eliot, Apostle of the North American Indians* (Boston, 1822). 174 p.

Contains Eliot's letters to Robert Boyle and other documents.

Oliphant, J. Orin, ed., *Through the South and West with Jeremiah Evarts in 1826* (Lewisburg, Pa., 1956). 143 p.

Evarts was the corresponding secretary of the American Board of Commissioners for Foreign Missions, and on this trip was surveying Indian missions in the south at a critical time. Oliphant's introduction contains an admirable account of Evarts' crusade against the Indian Removal Act of 1830, with valuable references to contemporary discussion of this issue.

Richardson, Leon Burr, ed., *An Indian Preacher in England: Being Letters and Diaries Relating to the Mission of the Reverend Samson Occom and the Reverend Nathaniel Whitaker to Collect Funds in England for the Benefit of Eleazar Wheelock's Indian Charity*

School, from Which Grew Dartmouth College (Hanover, N. H., 1933). 376 p., illus.
    From originals in Dartmouth Coll. MSS.

Shea, J. D. G., *History of the Catholic Missions among the Indian Tribes of the United States, 1529-1854* (N. Y., 1855). 514 p., illus.

Strong, William E., *The Story of the American Board* (Boston, 1910). 523 p., maps, illus.
    History of the American Board of Commissioners for Foreign Missions; contains much on missionary activities among Indians.

Tracy, Ebenezer C., *Memoir of the Life of Jeremiah Evarts* (Boston, 1845). 448 p.
    Evarts was secretary of the American Board of Commissioners for Foreign Missions and traveled extensively among the southern tribes; he was a vigorous opponent of Jackson's removal policy.

Trumbull, James Hammond, "The Indian Tongue and Its Literature as Fashioned by Eliot and Others," in Justin Winsor, ed., *The Memorial History of Boston* (Boston, 1880-1881), I, 465-480.

Trumbull, James Hammond, *Origin and Early Progress of Indian Missions in New England, with a List of Books in the Indian Language Printed at Cambridge and Boston, 1653-1721* (Worcester, 1874). 50 p.
    Repr. from Amer. Antiq. Soc., *Procs. . . . at the Annual Meeting,* Oct. 22, 1873.

Weis, Frederick Lewis, *The Society for Propagating the Gospel among the Indians and Others in North America, Incorporated 19 November 1787* (Dublin, N. H., 1953). 30 p.
    Contains an historical sketch, list of publications, etc. The MS records of the Society are complete from its first meeting.

Wheelock, Eleazar, *A Plain and Faithful Narrative of the Original Design, Rise, Progress and Present State of the Indian Charity-School at Lebanon, in Connecticut* (Boston, 1763), with several *Continuations* to 1775; a list is given in McCallum's *Wheelock,* pp. 218-219; Field 1638-1645.

[Wright, Asher] *Go'wăna gwa'ih sat'hah Yon de'yăs dah' gwah. A Spelling-book in the Seneca Language: with English Definitions* (Buffalo-Creek Reservation, Mission Press, 1842). 112 p.

Zeisberger, David, *Diary,* ed. Eugene F. Bliss (Cincinnati, 1885). 2 vols.

F. Government Policy

Abbott, Martin, "Indian Policy and Management in the Mississippi Territory, 1798-1817," *Jour. of Mississippi Hist.,* 14 (1952), 153-169.

Abel, Annie H., *The History of Events Resulting in Indian Consolidation West of the Mississippi River,* Amer. Hist. Assoc., *Ann. Report,* 1906, I (Wash., 1908), 233-250.

> Contains a valuable bibliographical supplement, pp. 413-438.

Abel, Annie H., "Proposals for an Indian State, 1778-1878," Amer. Hist. Assoc., *Ann. Report,* 1907, I (Wash., 1908), 87-104.

Alden, John Richard, *John Stuart and the Southern Colonial Frontier: A Study of Indian Relations, War, Trade, and Land Problems in the Southern Wilderness, 1754-1775* (Ann Arbor, 1944). 384 p., maps, bibliog.

Boyd, Julian P., "Dr. Franklin: Friend of the Indians," Franklin Inst., *Jour.,* 234 (1942), 311-330.

Brinton, Ellen Starr, "Benjamin West's Painting of Penn's Treaty with the Indians," Friends' Hist. Assoc., *Bull.,* 30 (1941), 99-166, illus.

> An exhaustive study of the famous painting of William Penn and the Indians at Shackamaxon on the Delaware (now part of Phila.) and of its historical and legendary background. The voluminous literature on Penn and the Indians is cited in footnotes.

[Cass, Lewis], "Considerations on the Present State of the Indians, and Their Removal to the West of the Mississippi," *North Amer. Rev.,* 30 (1830), 62-121.

[Cass, Lewis], "Remarks on the Policy and Practice of the United States and Great Britain in Their Treatment of the Indians," *North Amer. Rev.,* 24 (1827), 365-442.

> Also issued separately (Boston, 1827). 78 p.

Craven, Wesley Frank, "Indian Policy in Early Virginia," *William & Mary Quart.,* 3d ser., 1 (1944), 65-82.

Cohen, Felix S., *Handbook of Federal Indian Law* (Wash., 1941). 662 p., map, bibliog., index.

> Fourth printing 1945. Prepared within and for the U. S. Department of the Interior. A landmark in the understanding of the legal status of the Indian. Digests 400 treaties and 5,000 federal statutes dealing with Indian relations.

Dawson, Moses, *A Historical Narrative of the Civil and Military Services of Major-General William H. Harrison* ... (Cincinnati, 1824). 464 p.

Eisinger, Chester E., "The Puritans' Justification for Taking the Land," Essex Inst., *Historical Colls.*, 84 (1948), 131-143.

[Evarts, Jeremiah], *Essays on the Present Crisis in the Condition of the American Indian; First Published in the National Intelligencer, under the Signature of William Penn* (Boston, 1829). 112 p.

    Another edn., Phila., 1830. Opposing Jackson's Removal policy.

[Evarts, Jeremiah, ed.], *Speeches on the Passage of the Bill for the Removal of the Indians, Delivered in the Congress of the United States, April and May, 1830* (Boston and N. Y., 1830). 304 p.

    Speeches in Senate and House against the Indian Removal Bill, principally by Northerners (though David Crockett of Tennessee also spoke against the bill in a brief but characteristic speech), with a short introduction summarizing the arguments of speakers *for* the bill, which passed.

Farrand, Max, "The Indian Boundary Line [of 1763]," *Amer. Hist. Rev.*, 10 (1905), 782-791.

Finley, James B., *Life among the Indians; or, Personal Reminiscences and Historical Incidents Illustrative of Indian Life and Character* (Cincinnati, 1857). 548 p., illus.

    Finley was a Methodist missionary among the Wyandotts in Ohio.

Foreman, Grant, *Indian Removal: The Emigration of the Five Civilized Tribes* (Norman, Okla., 1932). 415 p., maps, illus., bibliog.

Foreman, Grant, *The Last Trek of the Indians* (Chicago, 1946). 382 p., maps, bibliog.

    Relates to removal of Eastern tribes other than the Five Civilized Tribes, dealt with in Foreman's *Indian Removal* (1932).

[Franklin, Benjamin], *A Narrative of the Late Massacres, in Lancaster County, of a Number of Indians, Friends of This Province, by Persons Unknown. With Some Observations on the Same* (Phila., 1764). 31 p.

    The most famous of the numerous tracts relating to the Paxton Boys affair. Available in several editions of Franklin's writings.

Gage, Thomas, *Correspondence . . . with the Secretaries of State, 1763-1775,* ed. Clarence E. Carter (New Haven, 1931-1933). 2 vols.

Vol. II contains also correspondence with the War Office, Treasury, and other officials.

Green, James A., *William Henry Harrison: His Life and Times* (Richmond, 1941). 536 p., illus., bibliog.

Hanke, Lewis, *The First Social Experiments in America: A Study in the Development of Spanish Indian Policy in the Sixteenth Century* (Cambridge, Mass., 1935). 99 p., bibliog.

Hanke, Lewis, *The Spanish Struggle for Justice in the Conquest of America* (Phila., 1949). 217 p., maps, illus., bibliog.

Prof. Hanke's studies of Spanish-Indian relations provide a valuable background to studies of English-Indian relations.

Harmon, George D., *Sixty Years of Indian Affairs, Political, Economic, and Diplomatic, 1789-1850* (Chapel Hill, 1941). 428 p., bibliog.

Part 1, The Formative Period, 1789-1825; Part 2, The Coercive Period, 1825-1850; Part 3, The Federal Government as the Guardian of the Indian.

Hawkins, Benjamin, *Letters . . . , 1796-1806,* Ga. Hist. Soc., *Colls.,* 9 (1916). 500 p.

Hawkins' "Sketch of the Creek Country in the Years 1798 and 1799" was published in *ibid.,* 3 (1848).

Hindle, Brooke, "The March of the Paxton Boys," *William and Mary Quart.,* 3d ser., 3 (1946), 461-486.

Hough, Franklin B., ed., *Proceedings of the Commissioners of Indian Affairs, Appointed by Law for the Extinguishment of Indian Titles in the State of New York* (Albany, 1861). 498 p., maps, illus.

Also published in 2 vols. *Munsell's Historical Series* (1861), IX-X. Covers period 1784-1790.

Jacobs, Wilbur R., ed., *Indians of the Southern Colonial Frontier: The Edmond Atkin Report and Plan of 1755* (Columbia, S. C., 1954). 108 p., maps, illus., facsims.

Edmond Atkin, a member of the governor's council of South Carolina, wrote an excellent plan for conduct of Indian affairs in the Southern Department. Had it worked, Atkin, like Sir William Johnson in the Northern Department, might have attained fame and fortune.

Jackson, Helen Hunt, *A Century of Dishonor: A Sketch of the United States Government's Dealings with Some of the Indian Tribes* (N. Y., 1881). 457 p.

> Among the tribes discussed are the Delawares and the Cherokees.

Kroeber, Alfred L., "Nature of the Land-Holding Group," *Ethnohistory, 2* (1955), 303-314.

> Puts forward the proposition that more often than not in native North America the land-owning and sovereign political society was not what we usually call "the tribe," but smaller units. "The tribe" is seen as a concept created by the whites in an effort to organize their dealings with the Indians.

McKenney, Thomas L., *Memoirs, Official and Personal; with Sketches of Travels among the Northern and Southern Indians* (N. Y., 1846). 2 vols. in 1, illus.

> McKenney was a federal Indian administrator and agent under Monroe and J. Q. Adams; he opposed the Removal policy and was dismissed by Jackson, but continued his activity in behalf of the Indians.

McLaughlin, Andrew C., "The Influence of Governor Cass on the Development of the Northwest," Amer. Hist. Assoc., *Papers, 3* (1889), 311-327.

Macleod, William Christie, *The American Indian Frontier* (N. Y., 1928). 598 p., maps, bibliog.

Manley, Henry S., *The Treaty of Fort Stanwix, 1784* (Rome, N. Y., 1932). 126 p., bibliog.

Marshe, Witham, *Lancaster in 1744: Journal of the Treaty at Lancaster in 1744, with the Six Nations,* ed. William H. Egle (Lancaster, 1884). 30 p.

> Also in Mass. Hist. Soc., *Colls.,* 1st ser., 7 (1800), 171-201.

Mohr, Walter H., *Federal Indian Relations, 1774-1788* (Phila., 1933). 247 p., map, bibliog.

Morse, Jedidiah, *A Report to the Secretary of War of the United States, on Indian Affairs, Comprising a Narrative of a Tour Performed in the Summer of 1820 . . . for the Purpose of Ascertaining, for the Use of the Government, the Actual State of the Indian Tribes in Our Country* (New Haven, 1822). 400 p., map, tables.

A valuable report prepared at the behest of Secretary of War John C. Calhoun. In making his extensive survey Morse was also acting under commissions from two missionary societies.

Parker, Thomas Valentine, *The Cherokee Indians* (N. Y., 1907). 116 p., map, illus., bibliog.

"A minute account of Cherokee relations with the Federal government prior to removal" (Starkey, *Cherokee Nation*).

Peake, Ora Brooks, *A History of the United States Indian Factory System, 1795-1822* (Denver, 1954). 340 p., map, illus., bibliog.

Based primarily on records in the National Archives.

Peters, Richard, *The Case of the Cherokee Nation against the State of Georgia* (Phila., 1831).

"A repository of memorials and documents relevant to the Removal Bill and the Cherokee Supreme Court case" (Starkey, *Cherokee Nation*).

Phillips, Ulrich B., *Georgia and State Rights,* Amer. Hist. Assoc., *Ann. Report,* 1901, II (Wash., 1902), 3-224.

Georgia, the Federal Government, and Indian removal.

Pound, Arthur, *Johnson of the Mohawks: A Biography of Sir William Johnson* (N. Y., 1930). 556 p., illus.

For a valuable commentary (and warning) about earlier biographies of Johnson, see Milton W. Hamilton, "Myths and Legends of Sir William Johnson," *N. Y. Hist.,* 34 (1953), 3-26.

Pound, Merritt B., *Benjamin Hawkins, Indian Agent* (Athens, Ga., 1951). 270 p., map, bibliog.

Royce, Charles C., comp., *Indian Land Cessions in the United States,* Bur. Amer. Ethnol., 18th *Ann. Report,* 1896-1897, pt. 2 (Wash., 1899), 521-997, 67 maps.

The Introduction (pp. 527-644), by Cyrus Thomas, reviews the Indian policy of Spain, France, and Great Britain; of the British North American colonies individually; and, briefly, of the United States. The cessions are arranged chronologically, 1784-1894, with historical notes. There is an index of tribes concerned in the cessions and a general index. The maps are arranged alphabetically by states.

Schmeckebier, Laurence F., *The Office of Indian Affairs: Its History, Activities and Organization* (Baltimore, 1927). 591 p., maps, bibliog.

A comprehensive account, with the early history of the Office and

its predecessors fully covered. Bibliography is extremely valuable
for its listing of pertinent government documents.

Shaw, Helen, *British Administration of the Southern Indians, 1756-
1783* (Lancaster, Penna., 1931). 205 p., bibliog.

Silver, James W., "A Counter-Proposal to the Indian Removal Policy of
Andrew Jackson," *Jour. of Mississippi Hist.,* 4 (1942), 207-215.

General Edmund Pendleton Gaines, in command of the Southeastern frontier, 1815-1821, and, at times after 1821, in command of
the army in the West, was sympathetic to the efforts of the Indians
to defend their rights to the land.

Thayer, Theodore, "The Friendly Association," *Penna. Mag. of Hist.,*
67 (1943), 356-376.

The Quakers and Indian policy in 18th-century Pennsylvania.

Thomson, Charles, *An Enquiry into the Causes of the Alienation of
the Delaware and Shawanese Indians from the British Interest, and
into the Measures Taken for Recovering Their Friendship* (London, 1759). 184 p., map.

Includes journal of Christian Frederick Post's mission to the
Ohio Indians, 1758, and other documents on Pennsylvania's Indian
relations.

Turner, Katherine C., *Red Men Calling on the Great White Father*
(Norman, Okla., 1951). 235 p., illus., bibliog.

Indian missions to the American seat of government, 1792-1911.

U. S. War Department, Office of Indian Affairs, *Reports* (Wash., 1824-
1848).

In 1849 the Office of Indian Affairs was transferred to the newly-
established Department of the Interior. From 1838 the *Reports* have
been issued by the Commissioner of the Office of Indian Affairs.
See note in Schmeckebier, *Office of Indian Affairs,* p. 547.

Volwiler, Albert T., *George Croghan and the Westward Movement,
1741-1782* (Cleveland, 1926). 370 p., maps, bibliog.

A new life of Croghan is in preparation by Nicholas B. Wain-
wright of the Historical Society of Pennsylvania.

Wallace, Paul A. W., *Conrad Weiser, 1696-1760: Friend of Colonist
and Mohawk* (Phila., 1945). 648 p.

One of the truly great source books on Six Nations history.

Wraxall, Peter, *An Abridgment of the Indian Affairs . . . Transacted*

in the Colony of New York, from the Year 1678 to the Year 1751,
ed. Charles H. McIlwain (Cambridge, Mass., 1915). 251 p.

The Introduction is an important study of the fur trade dominated by the Iroquois, and of Indian policy in colonial New York.

G. The Indian in Literature and Thought

Allen, Don Cameron, *The Legend of Noah: Renaissance Rationalism
in Art, Science, and Letters* (Urbana, Ill., 1949). 221 p., illus., bibliog.
   Discusses European conceptions of the origin and descent of the
American Indian, pp. 113-137.

Bissell, Benjamin, *The American Indian in English Literature of the
Eighteenth Century* (New Haven, 1925). 229 p., illus.

Chateaubriand, François Auguste René, vicomte de, *Les Natchez,* ed.
Gilbert Chinard (Baltimore and Paris, 1932). 554 p., map, illus.
   First published, Paris, 1826. The two first books of Chateaubriand's work, with a short introduction by Chinard, appeared in
the Univ. of Calif., *Pubns. in Mod. Philol.,* 7 (1919), 201-264. The
1932 edition contains a hundred-page introductory analysis by Chinard. The Natchez Indians made a profound impression on students
of early American history, and through Le Page du Pratz and
Chateaubriand on European literature and theories as to "man in
his integrity."

Chinard, Gilbert, *L'Amérique et le rêve exotique dans la littérature
française au XVIIe et au XVIIe siècle* (Paris, 1913). 448 p.
   Repr. 1934.

Chinard, Gilbert, *L'exotisme américain dans la littérature française au
XVIe siècle* (Paris, 1911). 246 p.

Drummond, A. M., and Richard Moody, "Indian Treaties: The First
American Dramas," *Quart. Jour. of Speech,* 39 (1953), 15-24.
   See also Wroth (§ VII, B).

Fairchild, Hoxie N., *The Noble Savage: A Study in Romantic Natural-
ism* (N. Y., 1928). 535 p., bibliog.
   Standard but inadequate work on the Indian and other "primi-
tives" in English literature of the 18th and early 19th centuries.

Grotius, Hugo, [1583-1645], *On the Origin of the Native Races of
America,* trans. and ed. Edmund Goldsmid (Edinburgh, 1884).
63 p.

Hallowell, Alfred Irving, "The Backwash of the Frontier: The Impact of the Indian on American Culture," in Walker D. Wyman and Clifton B. Kroeber, eds., *The Frontier in Perspective* (Madison: Univ. of Wisconsin Press, [1957?]).

The impact of the Indian on white society, an aspect of "acculturation" frequently overlooked, is a field of study offering excellent opportunities to the student of ethnohistory, especially to those approaching the subject from the historical or literary side. Prof. Hallowell, of the University of Pennsylvania, is one of those most actively engaged in research in the field, and his contribution to this forthcoming volume will be an important addition to the literature.

Horn, Georg, *De Originibus Americanis* (The Hague, 1652). 282 p.

Speculation on the origin of the Indians.

Keiser, Albert, *The Indian in American Literature* (N. Y., 1933). 312 p., bibliog.

Klingberg, Frank J., "The Noble Savage as Seen by the Missionary of the Society for the Propagation of the Gospel in Colonial New York, 1702-1750," Prot. Epis. Church in the U.S.A., *Historical Mag.,* 8 (1939), 128-165.

Parker, Arthur C., "Sources and Range of Cooper's Indian Lore," *New York Hist.,* 35 (1954), 447-456.

Pearce, Roy Harvey, *The Savages of America: A Study of the Indian and the Idea of Civilization* (Baltimore, 1953). 252 p.

A pioneering study of European-American attitudes toward the Indians from the period of discovery until the mid-19th century.

Powell, John H., "On the Origin of the American Indians," [An address delivered at the 131st Annual Meeting of The Athenaeum of Philadelphia, Feb. 4, 1946], (Phila., 1946). 24 p.

Richter, Conrad, *The Light in the Forest: A Novel* (N. Y., 1953). 179 p.

Fiction can sometimes capture the reality of the past better than history. Richter, in perusing colonial records, was "struck by the numbers of returned white captives who tried desperately to run away from their flesh-and-blood families and return to their Indian foster homes and the Indian mode of life." His novel explores the reasons for this attitude and throws light on the assumptions and beliefs underlying Indian and white societies.

Russell, Jason Almus, "The Indian in American Literature (1775-1875)," unpublished doctoral dissertation (Cornell, 1929).

> Superior to much that has been published on the subject. For published articles by Russell, see "Cooper: Interpreter of the Real and the Historical Indian," *Jour. Amer. Hist.*, 23 (1930), 41-71, and "The Narratives of Indian Captivities," *Education*, 51 (1930), 84-88.

Seeber, Edward D., "Critical Views on Logan's Speech," *Jour. Amer. Folklore*, 60 (1947), 130-146.

> An examination of the historicity of Chief Logan's famous 1774 speech to Lord Dunmore and its great influence in later American literature, politics, and education.

Smith, Samuel Stanhope, *An Essay on the Causes of the Variety of Complexion and Figure in the Human Species* . . . (New Brunswick, [N. J.], 1810). 411 p.

> First published 1787. 2d edn., enl., 1810, includes an Appendix, pp. 353-411, "Of the Natural Bravery and Fortitude of the American Indian. . . ."

Wallace, Paul A. W., "Cooper's Indians," *New York Hist.*, 35 (1954), 423-446.

Wallace, Paul A. W., "John Heckewelder's Indians and the Fenimore Cooper Tradition," Amer. Philos. Soc., *Procs.*, 96 (1952), 496-504.

Index

INDEX

Since the subject-matter of this book is Indians, no entries will be found under this word.